1968

This book may be kept

FOURTEEN DAYS

A fine will be charged for each day the book is kept overtime.

MR 2 7 '69			
GAYLORD 142			PRINTED IN U.S.A.

THE INTERVAL OF FREEDOM

INTERVAL OF *Freedom*

SOVIET LITERATURE DURING THE THAW
1954–1957

> "Man is born to live, not to prepare for life. Life itself, the phenomenon of life, the gift of life, is so breathtakingly serious!"
> BORIS PASTERNAK, *Doctor Zhivago*

by George Gibian

THE UNIVERSITY OF *Minnesota* PRESS, MINNEAPOLIS

To My Parents

AUTHOR'S *Preface*

WHEN Boris Pasternak's *Doctor Zhivago* was published in Europe and America in 1957 and 1958, the Western world was astonished and elated. After forty years of Communist rule, a Russian author still had the talent and courage to write an admirable novel completely at variance with the dreary works usually associated with Soviet Russian literature.

Doctor Zhivago was an event of major international significance. It may be too early to be certain about the literary value of the novel, but it is possible to say now that the great importance of the novel as a manifesto is already established. The book is likely to go down in history as one of the outstanding documents of the human condition in the middle of the twentieth century. But *Doctor Zhivago* is not the only significant literary work (although it is probably artistically the best) to come out of Soviet Russia in recent years. During four extraordinary years, 1954 to 1957, from Stalin's death to the aftermath of the Hungarian Revolution, Soviet Russian authors were able to speak their minds with unusual freedom. It is the purpose of this study to examine various revelations made in Soviet literature during this "interval of freedom."

The great interest of the books with which we shall be dealing lies mainly in their subject matter and the authors' attitudes toward it, rather than in their artistic merits. From a purely literary point of view, many of the works differ little from the conventional Soviet productions, which by their manner can hardly be distinguished from the second-rate realistic writing of the nineteenth century. The government has been successful in isolating almost all Russian authors from the work of the men most responsible for what we consider modern literature in the West. It has kept them in ignorance of it, or at least it has not allowed them to show any sign of its influence. (Even Pasternak did not know the works of Franz Kafka, for example, until foreign visitors brought him copies several years after Stalin's death.) Soviet literature has continued to be unaffected by such men as Proust, Joyce, Kafka, T. S. Eliot, D. H. Lawrence, Freud, and even now presents but little evidence that Russian writers are aware of their own nonrealistic literary heritage, the futurism of the early Mayakovsky, the symbolism of Bely or Blok.

Yet what Russian writers had to say from 1954 to 1957 has considerable interest and significance. They took advantage of the opportunity to speak on the questions which seemed the most important to them. Thus, through examining their literary productions, the world outside of Soviet Russia is enabled to gain insight into what agitates Soviet literary intellectuals, who are one of the most articulate and best informed groups in Russia and also most eager to express their opinions of the life around them.

We, in the West, can eavesdrop on this relatively free debate held by the Communist East with itself.

The discussion here will be organized under the three topics which most preoccupy Soviet writers and which also afford us the best look into the workings of Soviet society and of the Russian intellectual's mind: first, science (including the scientist, research, engineering, technology); second, love and sex; third, the literary "villain" or, in Soviet critical terminology, the "negative character."

Why should these three subjects be chosen as the focal points of an analysis of Soviet literature? At first glance they may appear to be unrelated. However, the conclusions which can be drawn from the treatment of them by Russian writers are similar and quite closely connected. It is not so much that these three subjects were chosen as that they chose themselves. They are the most important and frequent themes of Soviet literature of recent years. Readers of Russian novels and plays encounter these subjects at every turn. It is impossible to avoid them; they are central and recurrent concerns of Soviet authors. These subjects, moreover, are not only excellent approaches to the thinking of Soviet writers; they are also intrinsically interesting.

After examining the various conceptions of science, love, and villainy, and considering separately the significance of Boris Pasternak's *Doctor Zhivago*, I shall try to summarize what separates and what links together the outlooks on life of Russian and Western writers. The division of the world into two political and social spheres is one of the central problems of our time. The information that we can glean from the Soviet literature of these four exceptionally free years casts some light on the differences and similarities between these two parts of the world and on what they might be able to learn from each other.

A few words ought to be said about the principle used in the selection of works cited to illustrate Soviet writers' opinions. I have tried to present a variety of points of view and to include a range of different attitudes. The procedure is usually to start with a work typical of the "conservative," or Stalinist, Party-line literature, and then to move from one non-Stalinist book or group of books to another, usually progressively more and more vehemently anti-Stalinist, critical, even iconoclastic.

If the representation of the unconventional, daring, "negative," or "critical" works is disproportionately high and that of the Party-line works low, there are two reasons. First, the best and most interesting books of the period are those which expressed views divergent from the Party's official doctrines and therefore aroused controversies. The timid, docile books, while statistically most numerous even in the period we are considering, are the dullest and weakest. Secondly, it is usually unnecessary to examine more than one Party-line book, since they are monotonously alike, parroting the same views in the same manner. The "negative" books are to some extent free expressions of individuals; they vary widely. Hence the bulk of this study is devoted to examples of the latter.

No doubt a Stalinist critic could complain that the resulting selection is weighted in favor of controversial or negative works. It *is* thus weighted, but, I feel, necessarily so.

Some other works (for example Panova's *The Seasons of the*

Year or Lvova's *Elena*) would have served the purpose as well as those which are examined, but it has not been my intention to include all the important books written during these years. I have tried instead to avoid duplication and overlapping. Selective rather than complete coverage has been my aim. Significantly, however, in the process of selecting the most interesting and apt illustrations of the three themes, science, love, and villainy, most of the outstanding works of 1954–1957 did become relevant and are discussed.

Since only a few of the books discussed are available in English, summaries and quotations from them are used more extensively than would be necessary if translations had been published. The bibliography lists those books which are available in English versions. Where passages are quoted from Soviet works, the translations are my own.

Some pages of this book are adapted or reproduced from articles and book reviews which I published in the *New Republic*, *Problems of Communism*, *Soviet Survey*, and the *Progressive*. I am grateful to the editors of those periodicals for permission to use the materials again here.

I should like to thank the American Philosophical Society, whose grant-in-aid enabled me to do some of the research on which this study is based; the Inter-University Committee on Travel Grants, which made it possible for me to visit the USSR in 1956 and to speak with Soviet writers, editors, critics, and teachers of literature; and the Elizabeth Edwards Chase Fund of Smith College, which helped cover part of the clerical costs of preparing the manuscript. I am grateful for the courteous and invaluable aid of the staff of the Neilson Library of Smith College, as well as of the New York Public Library and Widener Library of Harvard University. I should also like to acknowledge my great debt to Jeanne Sinnen, editor at the University of Minnesota Press, for her extremely useful suggestions. Mrs. Marjorie Ericksen typed the manuscript speedily and cheerfully.

GEORGE GIBIAN

Northampton, Massachusetts
September 1, 1959

TABLE OF *Contents*

THE INTERVAL OF FREEDOM

CHAPTER I

Freedom and Aftermath, 1953 TO 1958

IF SOMEONE familiar with the conditions which prevailed in Soviet literature and culture during the life of Stalin had been kept in complete ignorance of his death and the ensuing changes and then had been plunged into the midst of Moscow and Leningrad literary life in 1956, he would not have believed his eyes and ears. Between the years 1954 and 1957, opinions were expressed by Soviet writers which during the years of Stalin's rule would certainly have been repressed by the writers themselves — or by the men in charge of controlling Soviet cultural life.

After 1954, writers in the USSR found themselves able to speak with a freedom very unusual in Soviet Russian history about those matters which lay closest to their hearts. In later chapters we shall examine in some detail the revelations which the Soviet literary intelligentsia made in novels, short stories, and plays published during these years of the interval of freedom, particularly about three key topics — science and technology, love, and human evil. But the rarity of the opportunity which has been given us to gain insights into Soviet Russian thinking on a number of important subjects can best be appreciated if the literature of this period is first set against the background of the cultural situation which preceded it and that which followed.

The hallowed, if vague, spirit which since 1932 has officially dominated Soviet writing, music, painting, and the other arts is designated "socialist realism." Just what "socialist realism" is and what it is not are difficult to determine precisely. Soviet authors themselves have had troubles with its definition. At the 1954 Congress of Writers,

3

one Soviet author complained that foreign Communist writers who kept asking for a specific definition of socialist realism did not understand that an exact description of it could not possibly be supplied. The foreigners, the Russian said, expected something like a recipe which would read "Mix fifty parts of positive hero, five parts negative hero, one part social contradiction, one part inspired romanticism, one hundred parts distilled water." The only advice he was able to give them was to peruse many works of Soviet literature and absorb the spirit of socialist realism from their reading.

In official practice, socialist realism has meant writing on topics which are of current concern to the people as a whole. But the Communist Party is taken to be the best spokesman for the people, since, armed with Marxism, that clairvoyant instrument of social and historical analysis, it is the interpreter of events; hence whatever the Party indicates as a desirable topic becomes the subject about which novels ought to be written.

Negatively, under the tenets of socialist realism, Soviet authors are enjoined to avoid a number of practices: subjectivism, delving into individual psychology and dissecting motives, which constituted one of the glories of nineteenth-century Russian literature; experimentation with literary forms – any kind of innovation or avant-gardism; dwelling on the role of the individual instead of the group, the social class; departures from realism by the use of symbolism or any other technique suggestive of the modern and radical. Positively, authors are exhorted to stress the group, the "collective," and to represent the typical realistically and without distortion. They are to remember that the trend of Soviet development is upward; therefore, it is more realistic to stress the positive elements in the present situation because they are going to be the dominant forces in the future and hence are more "typical" even today, whereas the negative elements should be played down because they belong to the past and are doomed to extinction – the author's eyes should be averted from them. Contemporary subjects are favored. The smiling tractor-driver and the steelworker overfulfilling his assigned production quota are the typical heroes, the collective farm and the factory the common settings of the action. A general mood of optimism should

4

pervade the literary work. A socialist realist must be happy about things and basically cheerful in his outlook. Banal, nauseatingly stereotyped novels and plays have resulted from all these pressures; poetry has languished.

A few outstanding writers in the 1930's succeeded in producing first-rate work even under the domination of socialist realism and the supervision of the Union of Writers. Some of them sincerely believed in the aims of the Party, their personal goals coincided with the official, and conformity was not subjectively felt by them as servility but rather as freedom to do what they really wanted to do. Others did regard the "social command" as a command and not their own free will, but they were skillful enough as literary artists to conform and still produce successful works. Still others, a small group of whom Mikhail Sholokhov, the author of *The Quiet Don*, was one, were great enough writers with sufficiently established reputations to defy the ill-defined but mighty specter of socialist realism. Their works were accepted as if they belonged to the proper category, even though they did not really fit the mold.

The bulk of Soviet literature in the thirties, however, presents a spectacle of dreary, uninspired, conformist mediocrity.

World War II brought some changes. For the time being the writers' own aims did to a great extent coincide with those of the Party. National defense, furthering the war effort, became their common concern. Some moving poetry, a spate of effective war novels, and an impressive amount of stirring battlefield reportage were produced. The restrictions on literature were somewhat relaxed.

The spontaneity of these years did not survive the war by very long. In 1946 the Party organized an offensive against the more independent writers who had gained a foothold during the war. Zhdanov, then presumed to be Stalin's heir apparent, delivered blistering speeches against satirists like Mikhail Zoshchenko, subjective lyrical poets like Anna Akhmatova, and editors and officials who had had the temerity to allow the publication of the objectionable works. Drastic measures were taken. Editors of various magazines were replaced and many authors were sent to exile or to camps, from which some never returned. We now know that Jewish writers

5

were among those persecuted with particular vigor. Between 1946 and 1953, all literary independence and originality disappeared. In an atmosphere of rigid, humorless uniformity, writers were expected to deal with the proper subjects in the proper manner. Strict though capricious supervision and stern punishments rooted out all opposition. Those writers of independent stamp were fortunate who ceased publishing and withdrew into some quiet nonliterary job. The less fortunate ones were arrested and jailed or executed.

Stalin died in March 1953.

The first harbinger of future changes appeared in April in the person of Olga Berggolts, who published an article severely critical of recent Soviet production in her own field, lyrical poetry. To attack what the writers were doing was not uncommon under Stalin, but her grounds were the opposite of those on which the Party's spokesmen had been accustomed to lambaste uncomfortably unorthodox literary works. Olga Berggolts wrote that after she had given a poetry reading program, someone asked her whether she would not add something "lyrical." This gave her pause, for she thought she had been reciting lyrical poetry all evening. When she returned home, she re-examined not only the poems she had read on that occasion, but also the poems in the leading literary journals of Russia for the past year, only to find that she had been wrong and her audience right. No true lyrics were being written in Russia. What was missing from Soviet poetry was "the most important thing . . . humanity, the human being." She found poems about operators of road construction machinery, with characters described from the outside, but no "lyrical hero with his own individual relationship to events and to the landscape," no true personal emotion.

The cause of the trouble, Olga Berggolts was suggesting, was the official witch hunt against allegedly pessimistic or subjective feelings. Whenever a poet expressed anything other than complete joy and happiness, he was apt to be accused of decadence. No wonder lyrical poetry had vanished. Poems were being written about the external lives of cheerful heroes of agricultural or industrial production, not about the inner life of emotion and passion.

6

Olga Berggolts' frontal attack on one dogma of Soviet literature was followed by many others. Another woman poet, Vera Inber, attacked the "steamshovel" school of poetry and the official literary critics responsible for its dominance. In December Vladimir Pomerantsev published an essay entitled "On Sincerity in Literature," which caused an uproar and is still frequently cited in the Soviet press as an example of heterodoxy. Pomerantsev said quite simply that much of recent Russian literature was bad because the authors did not describe reality truly. They "varnished" it, smoothing over unpleasant facts, putting on the manner of a Panglossian cheerleader instead of writing about things as they are. They ought to allow themselves to be guided by their spontaneous, immediate reactions and emotions, Pomerantsev urged them. He praised "sincerity" in this sense as the proper method of the writer. By implication he was denouncing both the Party for undertaking to guide all literary activities and the writers for proving servile followers.

It is not surprising that a storm broke over Pomerantsev's article. He enjoyed some powerful support, however, among figures well established in the hierarchy of Soviet culture. One of them was Ilya Ehrenburg, a man who had returned to Russia after years of hobnobbing with the bohemian literary avant-garde of Paris and ever since had floated along with the main current of Soviet writing, successfully rounding every curve in the Party line, a skilled opportunist par excellence. He had written an article in October 1953, before Pomerantsev's essay, praising Western writers, particularly Hemingway and Steinbeck, and calling attention to the fact that Chekhov, Tolstoy, and Gorky had written without having their subjects prescribed for them. Ehrenburg took up a position on the side of creative freedom: "Books cannot be ordered or planned."

The battle was on. Supporters of the liberal trend recalled that even before Stalin had died, at the Nineteenth Party Congress, Malenkov, who was to succeed Stalin as Premier of the USSR, had criticized the unrealistic typed characters and schematic situations of Russian novels and had urged the creation of more lifelike plots with convincing characters and conflicts. His words had gone largely unheeded at the time, but acquired new significance with Stalin's

7

death, the growth of Malenkov's political power, and the general loosening of cultural restrictions.

The new views of what was permissible in literature were for understandable reasons expressed first in theoretical articles; these can be written quickly and their reception in Soviet Russia serves as an indication of what it is safe for creative writers to attempt in their plays and novels. Then, in 1954, several works were published in which the new broad interpretation of artistic freedom was applied in original works of drama and fiction.

L. Zorin's play *The Guests* challenged the stereotyped notions that there is no class structure in Russia, that the typical highly placed Communist officials work always for the good of all people, and that an evil person cannot be a representative product of the Soviet system. The play centers on a conflict between an "old Bolshevik," who had worked for the Revolution, selflessly devoting himself to its cause, and who was now living quietly in the country, and his son, a member of the new class of top officials. This young man, living in wealth and luxury, is the villain of the piece. The dramatist put the indictment of the corrupt son into the mouth of his father, who says in a dramatic confrontation: "I simply worked, without knowing the smell of power. But you have known its taste since childhood; and it has poisoned you. . . . The country has grown stronger, the people has become richer. It can afford to make the present of a home or a car — for a good man nothing is too good. But the bad part of it is that together with the good man, alongside the hard workers, imperceptibly, people like you have appeared: rank-conscious aristocrats, greedy and conceited, remote from the people."

Zorin showed the tragedy in the betrayal of the Revolution by men who claim to be its servants. He revealed the existence of a power-structure in Russia, with corrupt men occupying top positions, pampered by the system which they abuse instead of serving.

Noteworthy too was Viktor Nekrasov's novel *Home Town*. It did not infringe the political dogmas of socialist realism, but it was remarkable for the literary excellence of its opening parts, its presentation of the purely personal, individual side of human experience, and the crass realism with which it re-created the desolate life in ruined Kiev in the last stages of the war.

Another important work of the year was the first part of a novelette by Ilya Ehrenburg himself, the title of which, *The Thaw*, soon became — both inside and outside of Russia — the label for the easing of controls after Stalin's death, in literature as well as in other spheres of life, from consumer goods to the secret police.

The Thaw is a loosely knit book about conditions in a provincial town. Several things in it flaunted taboos of Stalinist literature. It made references to the anti-Semitic persecutions under Stalin (particularly the "doctors' plot"); to factory managers who disregarded the interests of the economy and of labor, chalking up records in the easiest branches of industrial production while consigning their workers to live in unsafe hovels; to truly gifted painters who devoted themselves to their art but were penalized by poverty and public neglect for their uncompromising standards, while opportunistic hacks who prostituted their limited talents to currently popular topics were being rewarded in prestige and money; and to the persecution of people with contacts abroad. Throughout the book runs a contrast between the deep freeze (literally, in the sense of climate, and figuratively, in the sense of Stalinist attitudes) and the thaw, welcomed as a relief by the characters and obviously also by the author, when both the season of the year and the political atmosphere changed with the coming of spring.

With perfect timing, Ehrenburg succeeded in expressing the general feeling that conditions were improving and that the future was going to be brighter — it might now be possible to admit that in the past many things in Soviet Russia had been far from ideal.

But the tough-line Union of Writers officials were still resisting the threatening tide of "formalistic" and "negative" writing. A meeting of the presidium of the Union of Writers was held in August, and in September, the magazine which had printed several of the iconoclastic articles, the *New World* (*Novy Mir*), was severely reprimanded. Its editor was replaced and a group of authors, including Pomerantsev, were accused of having wished "to revise the basic principles of Soviet literature and to throw its ideological content and

9

truthfulness into doubt . . . in contradiction to directives of the Party in the field of literature and forgetful of the decisions taken between 1946 and 1948."

Despite some temporary reverses, however, the trend was still toward greater freedom. One sign of the change was the number of rehabilitations of authors, both living and dead, who had previously been silenced and, as customary in Soviet Russia, decreed to be "unpersons" and eliminated from all records. Marina Tsvetaeva, Ivan Kataev, Vladimir Kirshon, Isaac Babel, Yuri Olesha, and Vsevolod Meyerhold were among those resurrected, in 1954 or later. The *émigré* Bunin, the previously half-tolerated, half-censored Dostoevsky, and numerous other such authors were reprinted, praised, frequently cited.

Many of the rehabilitations were handled in amusingly surreptitious fashion: the author's name would suddenly appear, perhaps buried in a long list of writers; or a little notice would be tucked away in the back pages of the newspapers stating that a commission had been named to investigate the "literary heritage" of the author and to prepare the publication of a selection of his works; or an edition of his writings might be put on sale. Often no reference at all was made to the author's earlier unfortunate fate. Only on a few occasions would it be mentioned that he had "perished after unfounded accusations." Whether anything was openly stated or not, the literary public understood what had happened to the authors in the years when they had disappeared from public view.*

* A personal experience may illustrate this process. In 1956, I had the opportunity to observe rehabilitation at work in Russia. I was traveling by train in a compartment with several Russians. One of them asked if he could borrow a new book he saw me reading, the first volume of *Literary Moscow*, published that summer, which contained some poems by Anna Akhmatova, Zhdanov's victim in 1946. He leafed through the book, and then, startled, turned to the other Russian passengers and said quietly but with a significant look: "They are printing Akhmatova!" Nothing further was said, no discussion followed, perhaps because of their fear of each other or uncertainty about my presence. But it was clear that an important fact had sunk in. No doubt each of them on arriving at home was going to spread the word: Akhmatova was all right again.

A few days earlier, I had been told in Moscow that the works of Isaac Babel, suppressed since the 1930's, would be published again. When I visited Odessa, his home town and the setting of some of his best stories, I asked about him. I met a wall of ignorance and silence. The word had not yet come down

The fate of Boris Pasternak's poems and novel belongs in part to the subject of rehabilitations, for while he had worked for years on translations from English, German, and other languages, and was widely known as a translator of Shakespeare, since the war he had not been able to publish any of his own excellent, difficult, reflective, totally un-socialist-realistic poetry. In the May 1954 issue of the magazine *Banner* (*Znamya*), a group of his poems, part of his novel *Doctor Zhivago*, were published. At that time it was apparently expected that the entire novel would be published in Russia.

One of the most encouraging features of Russian literary life during this period was the freedom with which a genuine debate could be carried on. It had been part of the nineteenth-century national tradition for Russians to be unrestrainedly vehement when arguing with an opponent in print. Under Stalin, however, while the attacker representing the Party line could use violent language, the victim could not reply in kind, much as he may have wished to. What were supposed to be discussions were in reality one-way denunciations. The novelty of 1954 was that now attacks could be answered. There were rebuttals and re-rebuttals. A genuine war was being waged between the opposing schools of thought, not only behind the scenes, but in public view and in print.

The best example of these free-wheeling controversies may be found in the discussions during the Congress of Writers held in December 1954.* What previously may have been secretly thought by some writers or spoken only in a conversation among trusted friends was now being said in public. Some authors asked for more democracy in the Union of Writers.† They declared that "the force of

---

from the capital to Odessa that Babel was being rehabilitated. I could find no trace of Babel, not even any evidence that he had ever lived. Of all the professors in the Russian and Ukrainian literature departments at the University of Odessa whom I asked about Babel, only one would admit that she ever heard of him — the best of the Odessa School in the twenties, at that time one of the two or three most famous writers in all of Soviet Russia.

Late in 1957 a fairly complete one-volume collection of Babel's works was published in Moscow, through which he has again become familiar to at least a narrow segment of the Russian literary public.

* The second of three USSR-wide congresses held thus far. (The first took place in 1934, the third in 1959.)

† The Union of Writers is the most important institution within the Soviet organizational structure of literature. It is also the Party's main means of

11

unanimity in our criticism, in essence a deeply positive thing, an example of Party solidarity, turns into its opposite, a negative thing." Others urged that more truly artistic, aesthetic literary criticism (as opposed to sociological comment on a work's contents) be practiced. Arguments raged over the nature of socialist realism. Ehrenburg was attacked for *The Thaw* and came back with the surprising statement that he agreed the novelette was defective, but not because it went too far. It did not go far enough: "If I write another book, I shall try to make it a step forward from my last novelette, not a step back."

Freedom of speech was not complete. Nobody challenged the two key doctrines of Soviet literature: Party control over literature and the exclusive rule of socialist realism. Still, the relatively free discussion of *how* the Party ought to guide literature, and *what* socialist realism is, constituted a more exhilarating, more democratic experience than anything that had happened in Soviet culture since the previous Writers' Congress in 1934.

Two important events outside the field of literature further intensified the cultural "thaw": the Geneva Conference in July 1955, which generated a spirit of good-will, benevolence, and toleration; and the Twentieth Communist Party Congress, in February 1956, with its slashing attacks on Stalin and Stalinism. At the Congress Nikita

---

controlling authors. From 1917 to 1928, a number of organizations with varying aims, programs, literary tendencies, and even degrees of acceptance of the Soviet state and the Communist Party, served to unite writers. In 1928 the Party made the Russian Association of Proletarian Writers the dominant organization, but, dissatisfied in its experience with this association, the Party dissolved it in 1932 and replaced it with the monopolistic Union of Writers. This organization is something of a mixture of guild, professional association, social club, and supervisory commission on behalf of the government. Membership in it is a sign of status as a professional writer. The Union publishes magazines, owns clubhouses and apartment houses in Moscow and summer houses and rest homes in the country, and organizes readings and discussions of new works. There is a central organization of the Union, as well as branches in the various republics of the USSR and in the major cities. Economic and professional advantages accrue from maintaining good standing in the Union of Writers. At the same time, through those members of the Union who are also card-holding members of the Communist Party and through links to the government (the Ministry of Culture) and to the Party (Central Committee), the Union of Writers serves as a very convenient instrument for conveying to writers what the Party line on literature is at any given time, forestalling the writing or publishing of unsatisfactory, objectionable works, and chastising dissident authors.

Khrushchev directed a special message to Soviet writers and artists: "Our country's arts and literature can and must seek to become the best in the world, not only in richness of content, but also in artistic power and skill. We cannot be reconciled, as are some comrades in art agencies, editorial offices, and publishing houses, to dull and hasty works."

Khrushchev's attitude, echoed in other Congress statements, encouraged many of the cultural intelligentsia to believe that the thaw was on in earnest, that the way was open to greater creative and intellectual freedom without bureaucratic interference. At the same time his more dynamic pronouncements on the "cult of personality" and his attack on Stalin (when it became known) both encouraged appraisals of what had been "wrong" with Soviet society and lessened the fear that honest answers would bring terroristic reprisal.

The expansive spirit of optimism which infected the intellectual leaders in the aftermath of the Congress manifested itself in various ways. Editors started publishing translations of foreign authors, including Saroyan and Hemingway. A host of new literary periodicals were started, among them the magazines *Moscow* (*Moskva*) and *Neva*, the almanac *Our Contemporary Review* (*Nash Sovremennik*), and *Foreign Literature* (*Inostrannaya Literatura*), a journal devoted to translations and critical discussion of foreign works, particularly exhilarating to Soviet readers.

The change in climate was reflected perhaps most clearly in the tenor and content of new creative output — the plays, novels, poems, and stories published in the summer and fall of 1956. Dozens of works expressed novel and provocative attitudes. A notable example was Z. Paperny's *Genya and Senya*, a brief dramatic sketch parodying the typical Soviet play based on the precepts of socialist realism. In a spirit of boisterous humor the playlet dared to satirize the stereotyped anticapitalistic propaganda expected of Soviet playwrights and poked fun at the favorite themes of Soviet drama — industrial inventions and collective farm life. S. Aleshin's play *Alone* caused a stir because of its sympathetic treatment of the individual's personal needs and desires in a situation of moral conflict — in this case a love triangle raising the problem of divorce.

13

Three works published in the *New World* in the fall of 1956 became the rallying points of the advocates of a new literature, as well as objects of attacks by the hard-line Party spokesmen. The first appeared in August, Daniel Granin's short story "Personal Convictions." Melancholy in mood, it is pessimistic in its view of Soviet social organization and its effects on human character. The September issue of the magazine contained a long poem by Semen Kirsanov, "The Seven Days of the Week." In this fantasy, the hero invents a new heart with which to replace the "petrified" hearts of Soviet citizens. The poem pillories the inhuman, unfeeling life of the people, as well as the indifference and callousness of the bureaucracy in its efforts to control human feelings. Three issues, August through October, brought out Vladimir Dudintsev's notable *Not by Bread Alone*. The novel became the focus of literary discussions not because it contributed something new, but rather for the opposite reason: it was a synthesis of revolutionary attitudes already — though usually more cautiously and moderately — expressed by other writers. Dudintsev took one of the party's favorite subjects, the technological novel about an inventor's struggles, and perverted it, breaking many of the canons of socialist realism. He shows the inventor as a lonely figure, facing numerous enemies; his hero has an affair with the wife of his antagonist; the villains of the novel are bureaucrats, men successful in the Soviet system, and they are still in power at the end of the book. In more detail than Granin, Dudintsev depicts the damage done to the integrity of Soviet citizens by the country's social system.

A large anthology entitled *The Day of Poetry* (*Den Poezii*) appeared late in 1956, containing poems by more than one hundred poets, as well as several provocative critical articles on poetic problems. Some of the poems are so subjective, purely lyrical, or modernistic that a few months earlier — or a few months later — they might have been condemned as "formalistic" deviations. They included poems by the late Marina Tsvetaeva, with an introduction admitting she "did not understand and did not accept the October Revolution," although the fact that she committed suicide after returning to the USSR from exile was omitted; satirical verses by

Z. Paperny; translations of two poems by Perets Markish, a Yiddish poet who perished during Soviet anti-Semitic persecutions; and works by Margarita Aliger and other poets who either were in disfavor before the volume's publication or later fell from grace. Several of the critical essays included in the anthology defended the poet's right to be individual, lyrical, and free in his writing. Discernible throughout the book is the enthusiasm of the period: the poet's "heart believes that we are on the eve of a new and perhaps unprecedented flowering of Soviet poetry," wrote one of the contributors optimistically. Unfortunately, no such flowering is yet in evidence.

Even more dramatic was the content of the second volume of the anthology *Literary Moscow* (*Literaturnaya Moskva*). The first volume, which appeared in the summer of 1956, included in addition to two poems by Anna Akhmatova, victim of Zhdanov's 1946 purge, works by the notorious "formalists" Boris Pasternak and Viktor Shklovsky; otherwise, however, it contained little that could disturb the party's watchdogs. The second volume, appearing later that year, was very different. It abounded in materials of such import as to make it a landmark in the history of Russian literature. The most important essay in the volume was "A Writer's Notes" by the dramatist A. Kron, who candidly analyzed the consequences of Stalinism as follows: "Where cult is present, scientific thought must give way to blind faith, creativity to dogma, public opinion to caprice. The cult gives birth to a hierarchy of servants of the cult — the deity must have worshipers and obsequiousness. The cult is incompatible with criticism; the healthiest criticism is easily twisted into a heresy. . . . Where the taste of one man becomes incontrovertible, a leveling down and a crude interference in the artistic process . . . are inevitable. Under those conditions, not to be understood meant to be condemned. Where one man owns the truth uncontrolled, artists are relegated to the modest role of illustrators and singers of odes."

A short story in the anthology, Nikolai Zhdanov's "A Trip Home," deals with the contrast between a Communist leader's view of life from his office and the conditions he actually finds on a collective farm. Alexander Yashin's "Levers" is an equally negative picture of country life. The author undermines the standing official myths: the

15

Communist Party he depicts knows little about the collective farmers' lives; it abuses and bosses them, treating them coldly and impersonally. Other notable pieces in *Literary Moscow* are a novel by Venyamin Kaverin, *Searches and Hopes*, presenting a critical view of Soviet biology and health institutes; two stories by Yuri Nagibin; and a satirical fable by Sergei Mikhalkov.

Looking only at the works described thus far, the landmarks of the post-Congress shift toward literary freedom, one might be led to think that the pre-Congress thaw was turning into a full-scale literary revolt against party precepts. However, we must remember that not all the works which expressed negative opinions were equally distasteful or hostile to the Party. Writers were encouraged or at least permitted by the Party to criticize within certain limited areas; there were targets which the Party regarded as needing a little literary investigation and chastisement, for example petty tyrants in the bureaucracy. Many such works remained within the fold and their authors in favor with the authorities. Only writing which went beyond the bounds of what the Party wanted exposed was officially condemned.

Moreover, throughout this period there was plenty of vocal opposition from the spokesmen for an orthodox literature, who sharply attacked the new literary works and urged tighter controls, a more positive depiction of Soviet life, and closer adherence to the Party line. In the course of most of 1956, these demands appeared to be a rear-guard action by outnumbered Stalinists. The Polish and Hungarian revolts, however, rallied the forces of repression into a powerful counterattack. The gradual shift in the critical balance of power can be seen by comparing literary discussions of October and November 1956 with later writers' meetings in March, May, and June 1957.

In October 1956, a number of noted critics and writers joined a Conference of Inventors, Efficiency Experts, and Production Innovators, to debate *Not by Bread Alone* — a unique event in literary history. The literary men seem to have done more talking on this occasion than the technical specialists in the subject matter of the novel. Author Konstantin Simonov, notably adept at supporting the predominant party view at a given moment (although his timing has sometimes been bad) was among those who attacked Dudintsev. He complained (quite rightly) that the novel appeared to criticize the entire party and state bureaucracy instead of depicting the "bad" bureaucrat, Drozdov, as only an isolated case whom all the healthy forces of Soviet Russia were combating. Others deplored the "terrible individualism and . . . hopelessness" of the novel. Yet there were also many supporters of Dudintsev who spoke on his behalf. The vigorous defense which Dudintsev enjoyed made this October meeting a demonstration of the literary thaw.

In November, a meeting of the Moscow Union of Writers debated conditions in drama. Many comments were highly critical of "Stalinist" plays. One speaker "considered one of the major troubles of drama to be that the dramatic hero has been made less active and less independent; playwrights must show a man who thinks independently." Another declared: "The cult of the individual was seriously harmful to Soviet art and especially to drama. The notorious no-conflict theory, which has caused us much damage, was a direct consequence of the cult of the individual. The atmosphere created in art and literature in past years also caused serious errors. . . . Because criticism of a play or a performance was not always well-founded we have often drawn hasty organizational conclusions; a play has been withdrawn from the repertory, its production has been made difficult."

The most radical suggestion made at this meeting was put forward by V. Gubarev, who advocated not merely broadening, or redefining, but abolishing socialist realism. While Gubarev was attacked by many critics and writers for his remarks, his viewpoint was at least reported and debated in the Soviet press.

After the turn of the year, the mood of the literary discussions changed. The Moscow Union of Writers' report about the November drama discussion was condemned in January for suggesting that "negative" works such as Zorin's *Guests*, which had previously been censured, should perhaps be reconsidered. Zorin was again charged with distorting reality, with making the high-ranking bureaucrat represent evil in an exaggerated form, as if it were rooted in the Soviet way of life. "This play was written from mistaken positions, the revival of which would be very damaging to our literature," one Party-line critic maintained.

At a meeting of the Board of the Moscow Union of Writers in March 1957, the greater liveliness of literature in 1956 was noted with satisfaction, but the praise was accompanied by "sharp criticism of work which gave a one-sided picture of the life and activity of our Soviet people," according to *Izvestiya*. Many speakers devoted comments to the "shortcomings" of Dudintsev's novel and of the short stories and poetry published in the second volume of *Literary Moscow*. A plenary session of the Moscow Union of Writers later that month was the occasion for a good deal of further debating. Kirsanov, Aliger, Kaverin, and Dudintsev all spoke in defense of their works and against the official report delivered by D. Eremin. Konstantin Simonov gave a speech which steered a conciliatory course between Dudintsev and his attackers; several other speakers urged calmness in judging the literary output of 1956; and some very sharp attacks were made on the writers who had offended against literary orthodoxy.

In the weeks following the March meeting, the vigor and volume of press attacks on Yashin, Granin, Dudintsev, and Kron increased steadily. By the time of the May meeting of the Board of the Moscow Union of Writers, the editors of *Literary Moscow* were the particular butts of attack. The timing of the publication of the second volume of their anthology had been unfortunate. The material had been collected before October 1, but printing was not completed until after the Hungarian revolt. Works which stretched to the utmost the relative ideological laxity of the summer of 1956 were now being judged by party officials frightened by the demonstration in Poland and Hungary that writers granted an inch would seek a far greater measure of freedom. The recalcitrant writers and editors were accused of helping the West. They were urged to recant. Their refusal to do so was called a misguided attempt at the "heroism of silence."

On May 13, Khrushchev himself addressed the writers, aligning himself with the critics of the rebels. Six days later he delivered a second speech which was followed by several hard-line articles in *Pravda* and *Izvestiya*. Errant writers who were party members came in for particular attack. On June 6, it was reported in the press: "A meeting of the Communist writers of Moscow [has] fully approved the resolution of the [May] plenary session of the Writers' Union and in turn condemned the factionalism of the editorial board of *Literary Moscow*, a factionalism of which, unfortunately, the Communist writers E. Kazakevich, V. Tendryakov, and V. Rudny [all on the editorial staff of the anthology] are also guilty. The meeting of Communists approved the decision of the Party committee of the Moscow writers' organization to expel V. Rudny from the Party committee and instructed the Party committee to take up the matter of the behavior of the Communist members of the editorial board of *Literary Moscow*."

The writers and editors under attack apparently put up a last-ditch fight. According to a report in the *Literary Gazette* (*Literaturnaya Gazeta*), also on June 6: "[Kaverin] spoke extremely one-sidedly about the work of the editorial board of *Literary Moscow*. He defended works published in the second volume. . . . In a speech of E. Kazakevich there was no sign of a wish to admit honestly the errors committed. . . . [A. Yashin] acted as if even by this time he could not be certain what was wrong with 'The Levers'." The *Literary Gazette* went on to accuse the recalcitrant writers and editors of secretly upholding a political platform "not in agreement with the policy of the party in the area of literature."

At a general meeting of Moscow writers on June 11, Kazakevich, Aliger, and Bek surrendered, recanting in person or by letter. Margarita Aliger's letter apparently was not fully satisfactory, however, since she continued to be attacked. Through the following weeks, writers' meetings were held in many cities, all stressing the need for an "atmosphere of unanimity." Even then boycotts took place: in Leningrad, it was reported, "Many important writers simply did not honor our meeting with their presence."

The Party Central Committee's meeting (June 22–29, 1957) which followed the Molotov-Malenkov group's effort to wrest power from Khrushchev momentarily interrupted the drive to tighten literary controls. But as soon as the political struggle was over, Khrushchev found time to return to the subject of literature. In his third speech of that year to the writers, delivered in early July, Khrushchev emphasized the primacy of Party guidance, rephrased the commonplaces of socialist realism, and personally attacked Dudintsev and Margarita Aliger for daring to defend works "in which ideas alien to us are surreptitiously introduced."

Khrushchev's three speeches on literature were published in abridged form at the end of August. Since then they have become a classic of Soviet literary orthodoxy. Numerous endorsements of his thesis and promises to obey his exhortations were published in newspapers and magazines; rehashes of the speeches and editorials emphasizing their importance continued to be printed for many months.

Organizational changes were made. A new unit of the Union of Writers was set up for the Russian Republic as a whole, with trusted personnel in powerful positions on the organizing committee; apparently the intention was to provide a counterpoise to the Moscow Union of Writers, which was the center of the liberal trend. The rebellious writers, moreover, were linked with the "anti-Party group" of politicians, on whom the blame fell for the precarious literary situation. Of the "anti-Party" leaders, Shepilov was accused of an "unprincipled conciliatory attitude toward clearly unhealthy phenomena," Kaganovich of "demagogically accusing good Ukrainian poets of nationalism," Malenkov of "vulgarizing statements about the typical."

Later, even the Soviet successes with ballistic missiles and satellites were enlisted in attacking "negative" writers. A contributor to *Neva*, for example, argued in reference to Dudintsev's hero Lopatkin: "If he, with his simple invention, because of conditions allegedly existing in our country, could do nothing to place it in the service of the people, then who placed the ballistic rocket recently into the service of our country, perhaps of all mankind?"

In October 1957 the Party organization of Moscow writers convened in a joint meeting with the Board of the USSR Union of Writers. The keynote address by Valentin Kataev was reported under the press headline WE ARE GRATEFUL TO THE PARTY, aptly describing the attitude which the meeting was supposed to encourage. Leonid Sobolev and Anatoly Sofronov, writers faithful to the Party line, spoke smugly, almost gloatingly, about the need for publications like *New World, Moscow,* and *Literary Moscow* to avoid errors like those they had committed in the past. A complete contrast to their remarks was the humble, but perhaps ironical, recantation of Margarita Aliger, delivered on the same occasion: "I committed a number of gross mistakes in my public work. . . . It is my peculiarity at times to substitute moral-ethical categories for political categories. . . . Obviously I must now be much more exacting with myself, liberate myself from a certain speculativeness. . . . All the work of a Soviet writer is political work, and to accomplish it honorably is possible only when one follows firmly the Party line and Party discipline."

Complete conformity had not been entirely achieved, however. Occasional critical and daring essays had still been appearing. Ilya Ehrenburg, for instance, in an article on "The Lessons of Stendhal" appearing in the early summer of 1957, stirred up a furor among Soviet critics by using a subtle discussion of the French novelist to cast aspersions on Soviet efforts to guide literature along narrow political paths. His essay contained long passages which, while ostensibly concerned with early nineteenth-century France, obviously alluded to contemporary Russia: "Important is not the personality of the tyrant, but the essence of the tyranny. . . . The experience of Stendhal not only refutes the errors of the remote past; it also dispels many present-day illusions which occasionally are put forward as immutable truths."

Works of fiction much like those under condemnation had continued to be published. Galina Nikolaeva's long novel *A Battle on the Way* brilliantly exposes bureaucracy and inefficiency on collective farms and in factories, delves into issues of personal love, refers to political and anti-Semitic persecutions, and is at the same time, in some sections, one of the most successful artistic achievements of any Soviet novelist in recent time. Nikolai Gorbunov's "The Mistake (A Professor's Monologue)" rivals Granin's "Personal Convictions" in its melancholy picture of an institution on which Soviet Russia prides itself — organized scholarship. A prominent geographer analyzes his life and finds his personal achievements as well as the entire academic field of geography to be failures, despite all appearances of success by Soviet standards.

Soviet literature on the whole came under a cloud. Moves to rehabilitate certain writers were slowed down or halted (affecting, among others, Tsvetaeva and Akhmatova). Critical articles reiterated and elaborated Khrushchev's keynote: "The party carries on a merciless struggle against the penetration into literature and art of the influences of alien ideology, against hostile attacks on socialistic culture."

To the resurgent old-line spokesmen in Soviet culture, it was natural to think of art in terms of military metaphors: they considered creative artists an army fighting for the advancement of communism with the special weapons of their chosen occupation. Characteristic was this statement by a Soviet artist in the *Literary Gazette*: "No, our Academy of the Arts is not an aereopagus of 'priests of the beautiful,' it is not a preserve of self-absorbed thought remote from life's battles. It is the command post of our art, a faithful helper to the Party, the storage battery of the will of the nation, which wishes to see our artists in its midst, participating in its deeds, dreams, and triumphs." The chain of mixed metaphors — command post, helper, storage battery — was typical of how Soviet authors, too, were now again being urged to think of their function in society.

Through most of 1957 a seesaw struggle went on between the "liberals" and the "tough-liners." Toward the end of the year, the tough-liners had won. The war was succeeded by an enforced truce which, however, resembled a negotiated armistice more than an unconditional surrender. Lines of demarcation were drawn. The approved positions — the liberties which were permitted, distinct from those judged excessive — were quite clearly defined.

The supporters of "negative" and "sincere" writing then gradually lapsed into silence. The dominant note of official literary opinion was exemplified in the reports of a meeting of the Moscow Union of Writers in January 1958. On one hand, the heretics of Dudintsev's persuasion were buried once more. On the other, a warning was also

22

issued to the old-line Stalinists not to imagine that their day had returned: "The work of the new Board [of the Moscow Union of Writers] must be fully subordinated to the tasks expressed in the documents of the Party about literature. . . . The Communist Party pointed to ideological errors contained in V. Dudintsev's novel and the works of some other authors. . . . The trouble is not that the works which are now unanimously condemned sharply criticized negative features of reality or circumstances, but in whose name the writers were criticizing. . . . Soviet literature is not now being called to return to the milk and honey land of conflictlessness. A different platform is uniting the artists of socialistic realism. That is the quality of synthesis at which the artist must aim, uniting in himself the ability to capture the dominant tendency of the development of reality and at the same time the ability to see precisely the obstacles which hinder development." In other words, to cut through the woolly jargon of Soviet literary criticism, bad features of Soviet life may be depicted, but only if they are set in a context which makes it quite clear that the writer is a supporter of the Soviet regime and is convinced that the general trend of developments in Russia is onward and upward.

A. Surkov, who frequently rides herd on the mavericks of Soviet literature, added at this meeting: "Unfortunately my hopes were not fulfilled that some comrades who hold extreme points of view would speak at this conference, not in order to cast ashes over their heads, but in order to say, gathering all their inner manliness, that from now on they will no longer make such mistakes."

To those in the audience who were being castigated for not making public confessions of error, the distinction between promising not to make any more mistakes and casting ashes over their heads may have seemed very dubious.

At the same meeting, five authors, including Surkov, Fedin, and Sobolev, three important spokesmen for orthodoxy, criticized the other wing, that of Stalinist extremism, by reporting unfavorably on a series of articles by A. Sofronov. Sofronov had attacked all the conventional culprits of recent years, from Dudintsev to Kirsanov. But he had gone too far in calling them "literary critics and epileptics" and praising the sentiment that "he who is not with us is against us." The official squelching of Sofronov was an admonition to the Stalinists which balanced the verdict passed on the revisionists.

Thus the leaders of the Union of Writers established a middle course. The dark side of Soviet life was to be admitted here and there into literature, but only if the over-all effect was rosy. Deviants, however, were not to be attacked so harshly as to cause them to disappear from the literary scene altogether. Aliger, Yashin, Dudintsev, and others were forced to recant, but their heads did not roll, nor was it made impossible for them to return to print, as long as their future works conformed to directives. The paternal bosom of the Party, it was made clear, was waiting for the return of its prodigal literary sons and daughters.

In the fall of 1958, there seemed to be some danger of a return to Stalinist extremism. The publication of Boris Pasternak's *Doctor Zhivago* in the West and the award of the Nobel Prize to its author in October 1958 were followed by a Soviet campaign of terror against Pasternak. (The novel and its reception in Soviet Russia are the subjects of Chapter V.) The possibility arose that other liberal authors who had not gone as far as Pasternak would also be swept away in the general persecution and that the Twenty-First Party Congress in January and February 1959 and the series of writers' meetings scheduled between January and May of 1959 would uphold the extremists, men like Surkov and Sobolev, who were trying to take advantage of the opportunity to attack all dissidents.

However, the dominant tone at these conferences turned out to be conciliatory and moderate. The main official speeches and declarations merely repeated and underlined the clichés of socialist realism. At the Twenty-First Congress, for example, this was done in a long speech by the poet Tvardovsky; at the Third Congress of the Union of Writers, in May 1959, by Khrushchev himself, who noted that writers must "elevate the ideological and artistic level of their works, continue to be active helpers of the Party and of the government in the task of Communist education of the workers, in the development of the multinational Soviet culture, in the formation of high aesthetic taste, in the propagation of the principles of Communist morality." Artists were often reminded of the Seven-Year Plan and called upon to be dutifully optimistic about the wonderful growth now to take place in Soviet Russia. *Pravda* remarked, for example, on May 18, 1959, on the eve of the Third Congress, that writers must "show in all his greatness and beauty man building a new world and reveal the riches of his spiritual life."

Nothing drastic was done about Pasternak. On the contrary, the door now seems open for him to apply for readmission to the Union of Writers, which might mean social pardon and financial salvation (since royalties from his translations would start pouring in again). A significant event was the election of Pasternak's neighbor Konstantin Fedin, one of the patriarchs of Soviet letters, to the important post of secretary of the Union of Writers, displacing the rabid, irreconcilable Surkov.

At the same Third Writers' Congress, Khrushchev, who again surrendered to the temptation to address the writers, gave a speech adorned with quotations from various poems, including a particularly atrocious and uplifting one, which he attributed to a childhood friend. He repeatedly admitted he was not a literary critic and hence should not try to tell writers how to write, and then proceeded to do so anyway. He also insisted several times that he did not want to name names, and then referred to many writers by name. In one of the most interesting passages he spoke of Dudintsev. He said he had read *Not by Bread Alone*; Mikoyan had read the book first and had recommended that he read it. Dudintsev, he said, was trying to attack several things in Soviet life which Khrushchev himself also disliked, but the novelist erred by "exaggerating and generalizing." Then Khrushchev went on: "Dudintsev never was and is not an opponent of the Soviet system." Thus one of the main culprits of 1956 has been cleared and reinstated, by the highest authority.

Khrushchev's speech was friendly and restrained. He attacked all extremes. Particularly striking was his tone. As if he were chatting at a cocktail party, he rambled back and forth, informally and humanly. His closeness to his audience, his carefree attitude of a man confiding in other men whom he considers on the same level as himself, contrasted not only with Stalin's Oriental aloofness and

25

self-elevation, but also with Khrushchev's own manner in his 1957 speeches to the writers, when he spoke to the point and in the fashion of a stern high school principal chiding the student assembly.

In May 1959, Khrushchev complained about the press of political work: "I have read some of the works published recently, but unfortunately too little. Not because I do not need to or do not wish to read. I probably read no less than you, but I read communications of ambassadors, notes of ministers of foreign affairs, I read what the president of the USA has said, what the Prime Minister of some country has said. Of such literature I read a lot more than of your works. Of course not because I love this literature more than your books, but because in my position it is impossible for me not to read it."

Khrushchev described his experiences with some books which he did have time to read: "You read and your eyes keep shutting. You want to read on because some comrades who read the book spoke of it and you want to form your own opinion of it, but it is hard going. Your eyes close again. In order to read the book anyway, sometimes you take a pin and prick yourself and in this way keep waking yourself up in order to read the book through to the end."

The writers themselves, Khrushchev said, must be responsible for literary criticism. They should not imagine that someone else will "come with two bags, in one of which he has candy, in the other bitter pills, and he will hand out a piece of candy to one man, two pieces to another, a bitter pill to a third. It will be better if you yourselves both hand out the candy and receive the pills, deciding yourselves when this must be done and to whom. . . . You may say, 'Criticize us, control us; if a work is wrong, don't print it.' But you know, it is not so easy to make out what should be printed and what should not. The easiest way out is to print nothing. Then no mistakes will be made and it will look as if the man who forbade the printing of books is an intelligent man. But that would be stupid."

"I am known to be a champion of corn," Khrushchev joked, and went on to compare the proper nurture of literature with the growing of corn. He rambled on off the cuff: "If I said things that were wrong, I think you will forgive me. I admit I was very excited and worried.

At first I had thought I should follow my prepared text. But you know my character. . . . I do not like to read, I like to talk. . . . To speak without a written text is a difficult task for a speaker. I was not insured against making slips of the tongue. Therefore I beg you not to be severe judges."

Khrushchev spoke as if his purpose was to show the writers that the government was full of good will toward them. Quite apart from the question of what the policy toward writers was going to be in reality, the fact that Khrushchev wished to create the impression of friendliness was significant. It was bound to encourage some feeling of relaxation among writers who had been trained by years of experience with devious and not so devious methods of Party control to detect the slightest changes in line and hence would have no trouble in interpreting the meaning of Khrushchev's tone, the election of Fedin, the remarks about Dudintsev, and the general tendency to set a middle-of-the-road course.

Another characteristic of Khrushchev's speech which sets it off sharply from the usual programmatic statements of Soviet officials is that it was amusing and interesting. The most pervasive quality of "important leading articles" in the *Literary Gazette* or *Pravda* and of speeches by officials of the Union of Writers is their length and dullness. The Soviet reader is overwhelmed with boredom. It is difficult to exaggerate the dullness of official Soviet literary life. Speeches on literature are repetitious, unimaginative, endless. The same exhortations about the role of the writer which first crop up in a Central Committee resolution will be cited, rephrased, elaborated in a Party secretary's speech, then quoted and paraphrased in the *Literary Gazette*. A desperate feeling that if one continues to read the long columns, one will drown in them or go mad overcomes not only Westerners but Russian readers as well. Hence Khrushchev's May speech, for all its lack of new ideas, stands out by contrast as a pleasurable, unique experience. The whimsical talk, spiced with indiscretions and hints of indiscretions, seemed to promise other, better things to come.

The interval of freedom may be over, but the public gestures of the Party toward writers — carefully and repeatedly conveying the

27

idea that the Party is to be regarded as friendly, although watchful and prepared to intervene with rigor — mean that conditions on the eve of the 1960's are far from being as bad as they had been before Stalin's death. The Party line on literature now seems to be fairly well stabilized. It is conceivable that the present settlement, not so liberal as it was in 1954–1956, not so narrow as it had been under Stalin, could continue for a long time without major changes.

CHAPTER II

The Scientist AS HERO, SAINT, AND MARTYR

IN AMERICAN LITERATURE science and the scientist are not subjects of very great prominence. For most Americans, when the topic of science in fiction is brought up in conversation, the vaguely disreputable category of "science fiction," which is often considered to border on the sensational, or visions of Superman, space ships, and rocket cartoons are likely to come to mind. Probably only a few will think of the works of the Englishman H. G. Wells, the French novels of Jules Verne, other Utopian or fantastic novels, or examples of recent American science fiction which are of high quality and deserve to be taken seriously.

Other subjects are recognized in our country as the novelists' usual stalking grounds — the decayed southern mansion and the family within it; the Civil War; World Wars I and II; college and university life; Chicago slums; the scandals of small New England towns; Connecticut suburbia; hipsters' haunts; the hitchhiking trips of beatniks. But not science. The works of the American novelist Mitchell Wilson, which deal with American physicists, are little known in his own country; they are a household word in Soviet Russia.

In Russia, on the other hand, many serious novels draw on science and technology for their subject matter. Examples are easy to find; in fact, it would be more accurate to say that they are difficult to avoid. The novels from which illustrations of scientists' portraits are drawn later in this chapter were not painstakingly sought out; they are among the most discussed, most read Russian novels of the

29

last few years. Science and technology are perhaps the most popular of all subjects for Russian novelists; thus in examining these novels — and the depictions of science and various attitudes toward science to be found in them — we are face to face with the typical, representative fare of millions of Russian readers, with opinions and scenes to which millions of them are exposed.

The topic with which we are concerned is held in the forefront of the Soviet citizen's attention not only through novels, but by many other means, literary and nonliterary. A wide range of reading material publicizes science, from nonfictional, scientific reporting to fictionalized forms of writing in which scientific content is slight and marginal.

Many observers in the last decade have confirmed the prominent place occupied in the Soviet Union by propaganda for science. *Scientist in Russia,* the account of Eric Ashby who spent a year in Moscow as Australian "science attaché," has been followed by others describing the many forms of exaltation of science. Exhibitions are held in parks and museums; school children annually compete in attempting to solve physics problems in "Olympic Games" conducted like elimination tournaments; thousands of lectures are given about science to various assemblies of factory laborers and collective farm workers. Films often take scientists and scientific work as their subjects — the researches of Pavlov, Michurin, and others. Soviet films have been produced about the life of various animals, the habits of foxes, for example, and the general subject of the mother love of animals. The few Walt Disney nature films which were imported into Russia enjoyed great popularity.

Hero worship of the scientists is carried to the point where the celebrations in newspapers on a given day — the hundredth anniversary of a scientist's birthday or death, for instance — resemble the commemorations of saints' days in Tsarist times. The newspapers devote pages to accounts of scientists' lives and achievements; the summaries of their researches and discoveries provide an education for the public and maintain the prestige of the scientist. Widows and children of prominent scientists are awarded pensions and outright gifts of large sums of money — all duly reported in the daily press.

Mechnikov and phagocytes, Timiryazev and photosynthesis, Michurin and plant breeding, Mendeleev and the periodic table, Lobachevsky and non-Euclidian geometry, were widely popularized among the Russian public by such journalistic attention, as was Tsiolkovsky, the pioneer of aeronautics, rockets, and space travel.

The prominence given to science by the public media of Soviet Russia is in part explainable by the need to industrialize a backward country. Soviet Russia, after the Revolution of 1917, possessed a relatively small body of experienced workers and an even smaller body of scientific personnel (though in proportion to its numbers remarkably rich in first-class minds). Once it embarked on a program of industrialization (which was implicit in Marxist theory as well as demanded pragmatically by the specific situation at hand in the devastated country), it had to foster by all means available a growth of interest in technology and science. For many Russians this meant making the transition from a pre-Reformation, pre-Enlightenment, pre-Industrial Revolution state of mind directly to the twentieth-century outlook on science. The electrification of the 1920's and the industrialization basic to the successive five-year plans were predicated on an ever-increasing supply of scientific personnel and an understanding of scientific principles among the masses. Since the end of World War II, the immediate need forcing the authorities to expand scientific training and foment enthusiasm for technology has become still more acute.

But there is another very important though intangible reason for the tremendous emphasis on science in Russia. In such places as the Museum of Atheism and History of Religion, in the former Kazan Cathedral in Leningrad, science is constantly counterpoised to religion. On the crudest level this antithesis leads to exhibits typified by a reproduction in the Leningrad museum of a medieval painting showing a deathbed scene and a dove flying out the window — with an inscription reading: "In the Middle Ages, people believed in the superstition that man had a soul and that after his death it flew away in the form of a bird. Modern anatomy and the researches of Pavlov have proved that there is no such thing as a soul." This out-simplifies, out-vulgarizes any village atheist, including Flaubert's M. Homais.

31

Soviet Marxism claims to be a method of scientific analysis of history which in turn enables those with a hand on the control lever to direct the course of history and human development in the future. Since Marxism purports to be a science, it regards all sciences as its allies (but reserves the right to deny the appellation of science to those pursuits of which it disapproves, for example psychoanalysis and resonance theory in chemistry, and to force others to comply with Marxism's own aims and dogmas). Science is not only supposed to have supplanted religion; it is itself deified by the official ideology of Soviet Russia. It is not merely one of various pursuits in life or a method confined to a limited sphere; it is the pervasive and all-embracing, all-powerful method. Those who propagandize it, therefore, are not mere entertainers. They have an important, a serious duty. Many of them, in fact, speak with the hushed, hallowed accents of the reverent religious worshiper — or with the fiery persuasion of the proselytizer.

This chapter will be concerned primarily with the manner in which science has been dramatized in fiction, but it will not be amiss first to mention another literary form important in this connection which might be called the Soviet science documentary. The proto-type of this group is, according to Soviet writers, *Rasskaz o velikom plane* (1930) by M. Ilin (pseudonym of Ilya Marshak); an English translation was published under the title *Moscow Has a Plan*. Ilin's book deals with the first Five-Year Plan, translating the statistics into numerous concrete images. Written simply and vividly, illustrated with many diagrams and pictures, it glorifies industrialization. Ilin gives many picturesque and surprising facts about the technology underlying modern industry, emphasizing the dramatic and unusual. Often starting a new section with a puzzle or paradox, the book seems to be addressing itself to the child or adult without much education, in a manner in many ways reminiscent of a good progressive elementary school textbook. There is no plot, but one little fact after another is presented. It is an encyclopedia of eulogies of the Five-Year Plan. As a recent Soviet literary historian put it, the book has "no story, no intrigue, no adventures, yet it is interesting to read."

There seems to be no hero — yet there is one, a strange one: "without a name, without last name, no age, no character, no face. Yet he has incomparable charm, fascination. Who was the hero of that amazing book? Figures? Facts? No — creative thought."

In the thirty years since Ilin, many books have been written in the same tradition. Their titles suggest their subject matter: A. Buyanov's *The Wonderful Atom*; B. Rozen's *In the World of Large Molecules*; Ya. Segal's *How Man Became Big*; M. Ivanovsky's *The Subjugated Atom*; V. Orlov's *About Bold Thought*; I. Peshkin's *How Steel Is Born*; D. Danin's *The Good Atom*. There are many such books in America — but mostly for children. In Soviet Russia, serious books for adults are published under titles such as these.

Outstanding is L. Uspensky's *A Word about Words*, a booklet supplied in the margins with witty pictures illustrating various points on linguistics. Etymology, grammar, theories of origin of language, and other philological topics are presented in simple, vivid, dramatic form, accessible to anyone without specialized training, yet of great interest even to the specialist. It is a masterpiece of popularization done in a way not at all damaging to the accuracy and dignity of its scientific subject. (In Russian usage, science (*nauka*) is a far broader concept than in English. Somewhat like the Renaissance term *scientia*, it encompasses most branches of learning — the humanities as well as the social sciences; it is not restricted to the natural or physical sciences alone.)

A more conventional popularization of science is D. Dar's *Tale of Konstantine Tsiolkovsky*, written in 1946–1947, in which technology is presented in the guise of a biography. Tsiolkovsky, as well as Stalin and Soviet Russia, is fulsomely eulogized in this book, which more recently has been made into a stage play.

Characteristic of the Utopian romanticism of Soviet science documentaries (partly justified by demonstrable success in missile and satellite work) is Tsiolkovsky's radio address of May 1, 1933, quoted in the *Tale*. He is reported as having said that he had worked on propulsion rockets for forty years and had believed a trip to Mars would have to wait for many hundreds of years, but at the time of speaking, i.e. 1933, he had become convinced that many of those listening to his speech would live to witness interplanetary voyages. The book concludes with a quotation from one of Tsiolkovsky's last articles: "All I am saying is a weak attempt to foresee the future of aviation, aeronautics, and rocket propulsion. I am firmly convinced of one thing — the first place will belong to the Soviet Union. The capitalistic countries also work on these problems, but the capitalistic system hinders all that is new. Only in the Soviet Union do we have a powerful aviation industry, abundance of scientific institutions, concern on the part of society over problems of aeronautics, and an extraordinary love of all working people for their country, which assures the success of our undertakings."

After the death of Stalin, and still more after the Twentieth Party Congress, the Party relaxed its controls over the kind of science literature which could be published. The Party began to permit, perhaps even encouraged, writers to be more critical, more negative about bureaucratic rigidity, red tape, and various abuses in the institutional organization of science as well as about personal attitudes found in Soviet laboratories, institutes, and ministries. Its motive here was to use critical writing as a brush with which to sweep off the unhealthy growths within Soviet bureaucracy. The Party realized that a great deal was wrong in its scientific institutions. It intended to permit writers enough leeway to force the corruption into the open, to make people aware of what might be going on so that they would be on their guard against it, and also perhaps to shame or frighten the wrongdoers themselves.

The liberalization did not work out quite as the Party had hoped. Some writers went only as far as the Party wished them to, but others went further. Some used the limited freedom to break through various taboos of Soviet writing which were supposed to be still in force.

Of the examples that are examined here, three are Party-line books; one is on the borderline of the permitted and the dangerous; the last three are the most radical in their negative and critical attitude and in their — from the Party's point of view — *abuse* of the writer's privileges and freedoms. The last three are among those which have been most severely condemned by Soviet authorities.

First let us look at the conventional representation of a scientific subject in a book approved by the Party, propagandizing for and against exactly what the Party wishes to be praised or condemned: Alexander Bek's *The Life of Berezhkov* (published in *New World*, January–March 1956). In this somewhat unimaginative novel, which is very close to a documentary, an airplane engine designer, Alexei Berezhkov, tells the story of his career — of his work before 1917 and of the successive models of Soviet airplane motors he designed, with higher and higher horsepower. The novel is a linear tale of struggles against obstacles, ending with complete success. The author uses the technological subject to supply the suspense of a conflict between designer and recalcitrant nature, or between him and obtuse, ignorant, or ill-intentioned colleagues and superiors. The obstacles are never very formidable, however; one never doubts his ultimate success.

More significantly, the novel is a *Bildungsroman*, a didactic novel of the hero's growth and development. Berezhkov is taught a number of lessons in the course of his career. Bek presents him as first being educated in the rudiments of research: he must learn his own business, the designing of engines. Some of it consists of very elementary rules — not to duplicate what has already been done by other scientists, for example. Next he is trained more generally in personal virtues. The importance of modesty, understanding other people, and knowing how to learn from one's elders and superiors is brought home to him, each time through a telling incident.

The social education of Berezhkov is given the greatest stress. As a young man, he is oblivious to the social situation in his country and the place of his own work within it. When during World War I he helps build a vehicle called a "bat," with wheels ten meters high, which will knock down trees and pass over any terrain, a friend puts questions to him which awaken his sense of social responsibility. The friend asks first: Are people going to be happier because of your motor? Berezhkov answers that he wishes to show the world that a young Russian designer has built the best airplane and the best motor in the world. The same friend again asks him: Who is it that rules Russia? Berezhkov absorbs the implied suggestion that it is necessary to abolish the Tsarist system if inventions are to benefit the whole country.

After the Revolution, Berezhkov undergoes further education at the hands — literally — of children, members of the Young Communist League. Parts of these moralistic scenes are difficult for us to take seriously, but it seems that Bek intends them to be taken at their face value. For instance, the children first explain to the engineer that their greeting, a hand raised above the head, signifies that "social interests are higher than the personal." A girl Communist invites him to lecture on "the origin of life on earth" and when he suggests the subject of aviation development as closer to his field, the children reply, "One mustn't think only of oneself," and propose the topic "Aviation versus Religion." In the end they accept a lecture on the theme "How people fly and how they will fly in the future." But to make quite sure he has understood the principle with which they want to indoctrinate him, they leave with him this didactic parting advice: "Don't go too deeply into the technical side of it. Nowadays people of learning must pay attention to general questions of world outlook."

Berezhkov tells us that that he has learned on this occasion the lesson that "talent is obligation." But during the period of the New Economic Policy (inaugurated in 1921), he relapses from the upward line of his social growth by selling his services to a plant for 3000 rubles a month, a tremendous salary, far greater than most workers receive. His girl friend at this point becomes disillusioned with him — since his only explanation of why he is paid so much is that he has "the know-how." A government investigator questions him. It turns out that Berezhkov's conduct was perfectly legal, even if not socialistic. During the cross-examination Berezhkov reveals that he still takes the wrong attitude toward his exceptional gifts. "What about talent," he asks the investigator. "Is talent not power? In front of you is not an average man, in front of you is a man of extraordinary talent."

Through the mouth of the investigator — and through the mouth of Berezhkov himself as he recalls this in later years — the author condemns his attitude as individualistic and unsocial. The correct way, in Bek's mind, is to lend one's genius to socially useful ends, it being understood that the Party is the institution which puts the stamp of approval on what is and what is not a socially appropriate purpose.

Writers to be discussed later are worried by the problem of the exceptional man in society much more deeply than Bek, who disposes of it with great ease and emerges quite unruffled. He has a naive faith that the Party will find a suitable place for the exceptional man of genius and that no insurmountable problems will arise once the scientist realizes and accepts his proper role.

The major obstacles in Berezhkov's path, besides his own untutored self, are persons alien to Soviet society — not, we shall see below in Chapter IV, as in Dudintsev, Granin, and others, *typical*, native, Soviet characters. One of these obstacles is an American engineer, Weill, who invites Berezhkov to move to America and accept employment with his company. Berezhkov asks why he cannot work for the American company in Russia, producing engines there. Weill takes him to the window and points to the confusion of the market in front of the hotel. He tells Berezhkov that the scene is characteristic of the chaos reigning in Russia; one cannot build airplane motors in such a country. Weill's contempt for Russia — which he displays also in refusing to accept the measurements by Russian-built instruments which show that the imported American engines fall below the promised specifications — fans Berezhkov's nationalism still further.

Another obstacle, the head of a Ukrainian factory who refuses to produce one of Berezhkov's newly designed powerful motors, is Russian, but has close relations with foreign countries. He despises Russia and worships all that is foreign: "People like you and me must understand that in this hole we cannot produce motors such as are now being made abroad," he tells Berezhkov. To make it quite clear that the factory director is a despicable, negative character, Bek shows him admiring French art and culture in general — especially his favorite painting, Van Gogh's "Prisoners' Walk." "Who is there here [in Russia] who could have expressed the tragedy of life so

37

well?" the engineer asks — thus condemning himself by his own words as a decadent pessimist who sees only darkness or twilight in life.

In contrast, Berezhkov, as a proper, optimistic Soviet citizen, in accord with the Party's strictures on how to view life, looks at the cheerful side of things. The role of national pride and resentment of Russian technical inferiority as stimuli to scientific effort is shown by Berezhkov's reaction when he realizes that Soviet plants are having difficulties with 300-horsepower motors while foreign countries are producing far more powerful ones. Must he always study other people's designs, he asks himself when he is shown a glossy American magazine with illustrations of aviation engines and is asked to copy them so that they can be manufactured in Russia. "I wish American designers were studying photographs of my motor, our motor," he comments bitterly. The five-year plans are regarded in the novel as great opportunities for men with Berezhkov's nationalistic psychology to help Russia catch up with foreign countries, thus satisfying previously frustrated desires — a view which has direct bearing on the current extraordinary Soviet efforts in the industrial and scientific field. The joy with which Russians have welcomed their successes is based on their earlier impatience and humiliation brought on by constant copying of foreign achievements. Berezhkov's success in remedying Russian backwardness and surpassing the Westerners is presented as a triumph of wish-fulfillment.

Among other things which Bek emphasizes as important for Berezhkov to learn are the need to adapt his designs to the available production facilities (scientists must remember that their work should be of immediate practical usefulness and suitable for mass production); the proper view of Soviet living standards and consumer goods (contempt for the bathtubs which must be installed in foreign engineers' and instructors' houses — enthusiastic industrial effort is more important than "luxuries" which must wait until later); and discipline.

The necessity for discipline is illustrated when Berezhkov is sent on a mission to Leningrad. As soon as he arrives in that city, he solves in his head the main problems of designing a 1000-horsepower engine, a task of supreme importance. He goes immediately back to the airport, takes a special plane to Moscow, and taxis to his chief to report on his new ideas — without having completed his assignment in Leningrad. He is given a severe reprimand. His superior even dictates a letter of dismissal, which he cancels only after Berezhkov admits his guilt and shows an awareness of having offended against technological discipline.

On the other hand, the author sets an upper limit to passion for order, discipline, and smooth personal relations. Ordzhonikidze, the great industrial hero of this book, finds that the men charged with production of the 1000-horsepower motor designed by Berezhkov, who are having great difficulties with its production, have not asked Berezhkov to help them in their task. When he inquires why they have failed to use the brilliant designer, he is told that Berezhkov is individualistic, anarchistic, lacking in discipline. "It is more reasonable to do without his services," they tell Ordzhonikidze, who proceeds to scold them severely. "More reasonable?" he answers. "Perhaps quieter! I can imagine how Berezhkov would feel if he worked for a director like you" — and he installs Berezhkov as the head of all production.

In addition to this clear endorsement of Berezhkov's roughness and abruptness, as long as these traits do not lead to breach of discipline or insubordination, Bek also gives approval to Berezhkov's pride in his profession (when he is working not for his own profit but for social goals) and to his insistence on receiving what is his due as an engineer. Berezhkov requests sumptuous offices for himself as production engineer and is told that no one has ever asked for such offices before. He answers, "I am asking for them," and Bek applauds him. Now he is using his special gifts and training in the service of the country (unlike his pursuit of selfish aims in the NEP period); this changes the picture completely for the author. It is Berezhkov's duty to be demanding and to insist on receiving whatever will ease and advance his technical work. Berezhkov's aspirations as well as his requests are grandiose. There is a largeness, a broad sweep to his character.

Berezhkov is also encouraged to fight for his ideas. One must see one's projects through. He is told that he is the father of his engine; he must not abandon it even if it is necessary to go and see Ordzho-nikidze. Bek approves of boldness in the industrial struggle. The human type that is eulogized seems to be a return part way toward the rough ideal of the Revolutionary years. It is a step back from the Soviet version of the smooth man-in-gray-flannel-suit figure, the competent, friendly, suave, well-adjusted character whom we know from our own fiction, films, and life experience, a man who readily agrees, fits into a group smoothly, and is easy to get along with. The call now is for a rougher, more difficult person who is a more ener-getic scrapper.

Bek's novel strikes a Western reader as rather naive. It is a fast-paced, superficial account of the career of one man — of the obstacles he faces, his inner weakness, his gradual success in combating the enemy both within and without himself. The psychology is elemen-tary and obvious. Berezhkov's behavior is predictable. The author evidently constructed him according to a formula; the reader, too, quickly deduces what the formula is and can himself proceed to guess what Berezhkov will do next. The plot, then, as well as the concept of human nature, is simple and unoriginal. Yet the book has a cer-tain crude vigor. Its very lack of sophistication allows a brute force to be felt all the more immediately. If one is not repelled completely by the obviousness of the author's design on his readers, by his un-trameled and untamed didacticism to which no sacrifice seems to him too great, one may find oneself interested in the story as a Soviet version of a Horatio Alger myth — except that at the end, the hero becomes not a successful businessman, but a respected, socially in-spired, and socially conscious Soviet designer.

An entirely different branch of science forms the subject of Leonid Leonov's *The Russian Forest*, written between 1950 and 1953, and awarded the Lenin Prize in 1957. This book on the whole fulfills the Party's dream of a novel about scholarship or scientific work. Some sections, especially those set in prerevolutionary times, show flashes of the Leonov who wrote such great novels as *The Thief*, but for the most part this is not vintage Leonov; rather it is the work of a man who is trying very hard to write a novel acceptable to the authorities.

The novel contains a personal interest which complements the scientific — the inquiry of Polya Vikhrova, a simple country girl whose parents are separated, into the true nature of her father, Ivan Vikhrov, a professor of forestry in Moscow. She arrives in Moscow from the country at the beginning of World War II; she meets persons who know her father and talk about him without being aware that she is his daughter; she gradually comes to know him — and her country.

The scientific controversy consists of a long-drawn-out struggle between her father's views of the proper management of forests and those of his rival, Professor Gratsiansky. Ivan Vikhrov advocates slow, careful use of forests, with provision for replacement, forest-farming rather than exploitation. Gratsiansky has reviewed and ridiculed many of Vikhrov's books, without ever having contributed any work of his own: his is a purely negative, a destructive influence. He maintains that Soviet forests are so abundant that they can be exploited ruthlessly, at will, and that Vikhrov's attitude is a survival of the bourgeois way of thinking. In the end Vikhrov's views — and motives — are vindicated and Gratsiansky is exposed as a counter-revolutionary.

The struggles over forestry are as vehement as those over airplane engines in Bek's novel. Leonov, moreover, provides a rationale for sharp conflicts among Soviet scholars, defending their controversies as necessary and useful. One character says, "I am not apologizing for my directness. We are entering on a terrible period of unknown duration, the success of which is of greatest moment and will depend on the vigor with which the people will deal with each other." Hence conflicts between men holding opposed views *must* be sharp and open.

Such conflicts of necessity involve bitter confrontations of rivals and enemies. In Leonov's works, as well as in almost all the other novels and plays with which we are dealing, there is an abundance of characteristic climactic struggles (usually over questions of policy, industrial, agricultural, or professional).

Two kinds of scenes presenting sharp, dramatic arguments occur in most Soviet novels. One type consists of the protagonist's going to someone's office, usually his superior's, in plant, institute, or ministry, or the Party representative's. The protagonist's request is then discussed by the two men, across a desk. The second type is a crowd scene. A meeting is called, either by Party authorities or by the technicians, with Party representation, at which the disputed issues are to be decided. Speeches are made by supporters of both views — usually there are conservative or negative opinions opposed to the ideas of those requesting that something new be done; then, after much vigorous argument, often impugning the motives of the antagonists, a vote is taken and a decision made. Scenes of these two kinds constitute the focal points — the climaxes — of the agon, the struggle between the antagonistic sides. In Bek and Leonov, as well as in the authors who are about to be discussed, both types of scenes occur. The conventional pattern is followed by all of them almost without variation; but while their handling of the outward circumstances of these scenes is similar, the issues around which the battles rage may be quite different and the authors' attitudes completely at variance with one another.

Bek's subject, airplane engine design, is a field of technology superbly suited to the dramatization of urgency and speed — there is a constant surpassing of past accomplishments, for example in the climbing from 300 to 500 to 800 horsepower, with spectacular successes in the race against time. Leonov's field, forestry, on the other hand, is quite the opposite. It is a science requiring patience and the long view. Airplane motors may be obsolete before they have left the drawing table; the forester may not even live long enough to see the ultimate effects of his measures.

Leonov's novel has an illuminating passage showing the conventional Soviet ranking of various scientific fields in order of popularity: "Ivan had long ago become reconciled to the fact that among the occupations of his time, his own profession held one of the last places. All others — surgeons' work, geological surveying, the building of power plants, the gathering of unheard-of harvests without losses, the steering of naval vessels in an attack, the production of machines multiplying the number of working hands, the testing of experimental airplanes and thousands of other specialties — in people's opinion were justly regarded as heroic endeavors demanding boundless mental strain and valor. . . . The newspapers of the period were summoning men to feats of labor. In Professor Vikhrov's profession this was not possible. He was frequently reminded that the life expectation of foresters is the fourth highest, after beekeepers, priests, and gardeners, and their occupational disease is rheumatism, from which people do not die. For these reasons, Ivan occasionally felt painfully ill at ease when naming his occupation, as if he were the custodian of the Great Bear or the overseer of the beauties of the Black Sea."

What others find discouraging about his profession is what attracts Leonov's Professor Vikhrov to it. Like Chekhov's Doctor Astrov in *Uncle Vanya*, the professor dreams of work for future generations. To him long-range planning and the cooperation of several generations, far from being repellent, are the very essence of socialist idealism. Unlike Astrov, he does a great deal of practical work toward that end. A second important consideration for him is the connection between forestry and Russia — not as a political entity, but as a country. Forests become the symbol of his native land. Leonov associates them explicitly when he applies the expression "lost in the Russian forests" to the failure of the German invasion in World War II.

In Bek's novel, the negative side of nationalism is used as a spur to scientific effort. Bek's nationalism takes the form of anti-foreign feeling, resentment of foreign superiority, a wish to vindicate Russian honor and to show that what other nations can do, Russians are also able to do, as well or better. Leonov's nationalism is positive, without any element of animosity toward foreign nations or hurt pride. It is based on a love for Russian forests and, through them, love for the land — the natural resources of the country itself. Professor Vikhrov's introductory lecture in his course on forestry, reported at length in the book, is a paean in praise of Russian history and nature, rather than a mere routine classroom performance.

In the many novels which Leonov, one of the most interesting of the older generation of Soviet novelists, has written, love for Russia's past, her land, and her prerevolutionary traditions and folkways has often been prominent. *The Russian Forest*, the last in a long series of novels by this divided, backward-looking author, is consistent with his lifelong worship of his country's earth and natural beauty; it also shows his effort to accept the Party's preferences, for Leonov, while following his bent for delving into pre-1917 personalities and incidents, in this novel does so with emphasis on the black, gloomy, twisted, hostile elements of the past.

Daniel Granin, a young man just at the threshold of his literary career, was quite unbothered by either the historical background of Russia or her natural beauties when he wrote *Those Who Seek* between 1951 and 1954. Unlike most Soviet authors of books on science, he knows his subject from years of work in the field, since he is an engineer by training. Only after publishing a collection of short stories and this novel did he become a professional writer.

The novel describes the struggles of an electrical engineer, Andrei Lobanov, who is trying to develop a leak-locator, an instrument to measure the distance to a break in a buried power line — a device which has been in the possession of Western engineers for a considerable time. The book relates his fortunes from the moment of his appointment as director of a research laboratory attached to an electric power works: his reforms, his conflicts with various opponents, and his adventures and ultimate success in developing the instrument. It is indeed difficult to imagine such a subject and such a hero in an American novel.

An important theme of scientific work which we have not previously encountered is present here: the tension between the pure theoretician and the practical worker in the field. Lobanov holds a candidate's degree, roughly equivalent to the American Ph.D. His laboratory is devoted to industrial, not pure, research. His colleagues feel general surprise at his accepting the assignment. The pure theorists regard Lobanov as a traitor to their cause. An older professor had set his heart on recruiting Lobanov into teaching; he is hurt and surprised by Lobanov's decision to work in an industrial laboratory. It is evident that a far stronger prejudice exists in Soviet Russia

44

against getting one's hand dirty, and *for* a purely white-collar or theoretical job, than in the United States. In prestige as well as salary, pure research, teaching, and theoretical work rank much higher than the pursuit of applied science. Lobanov is asked how he succeeded in keeping the higher salary to which his candidate's degree automatically entitled him as long as he worked for a university or pure research institute. Clearly it did not even occur to the questioner that Lobanov may have come to the laboratory without bringing his preferential salary with him. Lobanov answers that he suffered a loss of one thousand rubles a month when he took his new position but felt compensated for it by the opportunities to do research with the help of the facilities and personnel of the laboratory. For this attitude another character sarcastically calls him "an idealist."

Granin depicts Andrei as clearly destined to be a research man, even as a student. His professor could see that "Andrei was interested only in the mysterious, contradictory sides of [his favorite subjects]. . . . The lecturer only had to say, 'On this point, comrades, there are several different opinions; little research has been carried out in the field,' and Andrei would start digging into his books and staying behind in the laboratory in the evening. The unknown aroused in him a wild feeling of protest, of insatiable curiosity." But to be a theoretician, a man attracted by mysteries, is not considered praiseworthy without qualification and under any circumstances. Andrei is shown to need much training in the practical handling of men. He must learn to go on picnics with his subordinates, to remember the names of wives and children, to be a warm human being interested in other human beings, and to exhibit other-directed, extrovert virtues. By way of contrast to Lobanov, the novel presents negatively certain professors of engineering as excessively theoretical in their bent and unwilling to cooperate with the practical needs of industry; the author castigates them while praising Lobanov for his willingness to bridge the two realms. One professor is described as "apprehensive of breaking away from his well-ordered way of life, from academic work unhampered by time limits."

Like Berezhkov, Lobanov is praised for his intransigence and proper pride in his own and his colleagues' work. When he takes over the laboratory, he finds some of the personnel in fact working for other departments; he demands that all men on his table of organization work for his laboratory and under his control. He has his way and is admired for it by the author, even though his harsh demands alienate many powerful people.

He also fights ruthlessly against using his facilities and men to repair the personal radio sets of influential officials and to do general maintenance work for the power industry. His is a development laboratory, he repeats, which is not meant for humdrum repair jobs. This naturally brings him into conflicts with his superiors; previous directors of the laboratory had acquiesced in demands for such work. Lobanov does not hesitate to argue that his men are trained and rare specialists who should be used only for exacting work, not routine jobs.

His attitude, by American standards, smacks of pride and elitism. The Soviet author praises him for it and considers the attitude economically defensible — as proper pride and justified desire to conserve rare human resources.

The type of personality favored by Granin is further clarified at one public disputation in which Granin's sympathies are entirely on the side of the "clumsy" and "passionate" Lobanov, the rough, woolly, pugnacious, romantic hero, and against the smooth, sophisticated, civilized type from the new Soviet intelligentsia of technicians. After this meeting — at which Lobanov is outvoted fifteen to four — his opponent meets him outside and says to him in the best conciliatory tradition (which is in the American tradition, too): "Let's make a pact; however much we quarrel at work, outside of work we'll be friends as we always have been. I don't like mixing these things." And he offers Lobanov a ride in his car. Lobanov refuses the ride and tells him, "No, it won't work. If we're at odds in our work, we'll be at odds everywhere." Work is everything to him; disagreements over technology pervade life and cannot be compartmentalized and tamed. He is an all-or-nothing fighter; once when he meets a representative of those who have stopped struggling and surrendered, he tells this defeatist: "You're deserters. You are repulsive even to yourselves. I'd rather deal with your chief than with

46

you. At least I'd get some pleasure out of punching him in the jaw."

This novel also expounds what is and what is not the proper spur of a scientist's research. The antagonist of Lobanov tells him that "the regrettable difference between practical engineers and scientists" is that the years of effort and energy a scientist spends on a piece of apparatus are forgotten when later some other engineer improves it further: "Soon the Lobanov instrument ceases to exist and instead it is Sidorov's, Petrov's, and so on. And no one remembers Lobanov; all your work is forgotten." Lobanov answers: "As for my eternal fame, you're wasting your time worrying about that. . . . There is something more brilliant and more fruitful than any individual scientist, and that is science itself, that irresistible process that is carried on day by day by thousands of rank and file scientific workers." His opponent, then, erred in seeing only individual fame, that last infirmity of the noble mind, as the scientist's motive — the pleasure of having an instrument named after oneself — to which Lobanov counterpoised love of science, the enthusiasm for collective, if necessarily anonymous, scientific work: "If the locator is ever created, it will be created not by me, but by the laboratory as a whole. The time of the lonely individual is coming to an end. Especially in science. All the biggest problems are solved by teams. And in any case the idea of contrasting science and engineering is, as I see it, utterly ridiculous and harmful. One thing cannot develop without the other." Other Russian writers do not agree with Lobanov's contention that the collective effort is replacing the individual; Dudintsev and others present the lonely genius, the individual, as still carrying the burden.

The Life of Berezhkov, The Russian Forest, and *Those Who Seek* are very outspoken in their representation of adverse conditions in Russian scholarship. They show that there is much that must be corrected. They contain passages which by any set of standards, but particularly by those of Stalinist Russia, must be judged to be very frank, even negative. Yet it would be an error to consider them dissident or hostile to Soviet policy. Their authors are careful to supply a counterbalance to the critical and denunciatory portrayals — a

47

positive character, a hero, a refutation, a sign pointing to a way out, to a method of remedying the unsavory circumstances, and most important of all, an optimistic, happy ending. They comply with the Party's wish that writers provide healthy criticism of social abuses, particularly within the structure of Soviet science and technology.

With Venyamin Kaverin's *Searches and Hopes* (part of his novel *The Open Book*), printed in *Literary Moscow*, Vol. II, 1956, we move into the category of novels considered dubious or even dangerous by the Party. The novel deals with penicillin research, as its heroine, Tatyana Vlasenkova, struggles for facilities to develop a Soviet version of the drug. (In the later sections of *Searches and Hopes* another interest dominates the novel: the circumstances under which her husband Andrei is unjustly accused, sentenced, and finally released.) The action takes place between the early stages of World War II, with the Germans outside of Moscow, and New Year's Day of 1956.

Tekhnika i lyudi, technology and people, are the two things that Tatyana gathered in April 1942 for her laboratory — and they are the two axes around which the novel revolves. Tatyana's serious troubles begin when she completes exploratory efforts to develop penicillin. The first hints come during her visit, with a colleague, to Deputy Minister of Health Maximov. His office is most impressive; on his desk is a malachite inkwell set with a snake (the symbol of medicine) wreathed around it. They are received with "rude condescension." By delicate shadings of behavior, Maximov insults his visitors. He does not rise when they leave; he never even congratulates them on having developed penicillin, as they remark between themselves afterwards. He agrees it is time for Russia to set up a penicillin factory — the English are already building one — but his consent is vague. After leaving the deputy minister, Tatyana and her colleague enact an imaginary meeting with a deputy minister who behaves as they think he should — greets them with great joy, graciousness, and admiration, and offers them any help within his power. Not least important in their daydream is that he accompanies them all the way to the door. Recognition through politeness and a show of respect seems as important to the two penicillin researchers as material aid and help in requisitioning sausage factories for conversion to penicillin plants.

Kaverin does not show Tatyana reading English publications about penicillin or making any effort to acquire information about what is being done abroad in her field. Her effort seems stubbornly domestic, self-sufficient. At one point the author does mention that Tatyana reads a brief note in the *British Journal of Experimental Pathology*, signed by three names — including the renowned Alexander Fleming — which informs her that her idea is no longer exclusively her own. "You are late" is the painful refrain which buzzes through her head thereafter. However, she continues her work. Her motivation is patriotic as well as humanitarian: she thinks of the wounded in Stalingrad, in the crowded rows of hospital cots; of their question, "Where is the drug with which you would lighten our suffering?"; and of the remark of a doctor who said one or two hundred learned men ought to be gathered together and ordered to invent a miracle.

A new stage of the heroine's success is reached with the arrival in Russia of an Oxford professor of general pathology, Norcross. Norcross is eager to observe Soviet manufacture of penicillin. He also brings a certain amount of English penicillin with him. Kaverin is sarcastic about the lavish hospitality extended to the visitor. The long-neglected and unrewarded Russian pioneer of penicillin research is made to comment: "Quiet, polite, well-dressed men appeared and, calling themselves workers of the trust of restaurants, set in my study a table covered with a crisp tablecloth, white as snow. It was evidently a magic table, for with magic speed delicious dishes such as had not been seen for a long time appeared on it." The penicillin mold, which had been the Cinderella of science, Kaverin says, is now in the position of Cinderella after she has lost her slipper and all the princes are looking for her in order to offer her their hand and heart. So at the reception for Norcross, with great attention now being shown to penicillin, various men who earlier had thrown obstacles in the path of penicillin research appear sanctimoniously, as if to help celebrate and to give the impression of having been in favor of the project all along.

49

The arrival of the Englishman calls forth a scientific duel. Tatyana's opponent Kramov, who has been hindering her in her efforts (his machinations will be described in greater detail in Chapter IV), proposes that a competition be carried out between English and Soviet penicillin. His intention is malicious — to force Tatyana's hand: if she refuses the test, her Russian penicillin will be discredited before the Ministry of Health and her own workers; if she accepts, he hopes the famed Oxford product will prove its superiority and she will be humiliated. Tatyana accepts. Twelve patients with equally serious cases of blood poisoning are divided into two groups and treated by Oxford and Russian penicillin. The results are not fully conclusive, since, after much suspense, all the patients are found to be cured. But Tatyana is pleased, for the dosage had not been the same: the British used 100,000 units a day, the Russians only a tenth of that amount. The moral victory is hers.

The contest also enables Kaverin to fire an anti-American blast, through the mouth of the English visitor, who claims the Americans took over his invention for their own profit and now the British are forced to buy back American patents. "At present twenty-one firms in America are occupied with production of penicillin. They are twenty-one pirate vessels freely sailing the open seas. On the mast is the black flag with a skull and bones, on board yellow magic invented not by the pirates, but by the men of science."

The bureaucracy of Soviet science is criticized in the novel. A Russian scientist says after a visit to Sweden, "In Sweden the director of the institute receives you at his laboratory desk. . . . The director works with his hands and does not wear out his trousers at meetings," whereas in Russia "in a scientific research institute with one hundred and twenty people in it, twenty actually work in science and the others only take their pay, have their laboratory assistants do the work, use up animals, and take up room of which there is not enough anyway."

True love for science is frequently exemplified, contrasting with the misuse of science. For instance, the brother of Tatyana's husband Andrei, Professor Mitya Lvov, who has dysentery when the Germans occupy Rostov, flees but is captured. When he thinks he is on the point of dying in a German jail—for he refuses to go to Berlin to help the enemy—his last thought is of his theory on the causes of cancer. He writes it down on a few slips of paper and entrusts it to a fellow prisoner, with the words "I do not wish that these ideas which may benefit mankind should perish together with me." However, the devoted scientist is rescued and he is able to rejoin Andrei.

Kaverin's attitude toward the "nationalism of science" is curious. Through most of the book, he seems to be sharing the Soviet Russian scientific chauvinism. He is delighted by the superiority of Soviet penicillin to the British. To develop Soviet science—with an eye to applause from the rest of the world—is one of the motives of those scientists whom he praises. But toward the end of the book, his attitude changes. Now chauvinism becomes hateful and ridiculous to his positive characters: "Don't you see how all around us people have gone simply mad over Russian primacy? It will appear that we invented the moon and the stars, not to speak of penicillin. In the years after the war, we stood before a strange task: to prove that our medical science was developing with extraordinary speed, or at least more quickly than the science of other countries of the whole world. The biggest discoveries of the nineteenth and twentieth centuries were ours and nobody else's—this was affirmed in books and articles, in films and in the theater. Nobody noticed that through defense of fabricated, imaginary primacy, we lost the genuine one, won in tormented work and research. . . . None of us had the right to share his discoveries even with the neighbor's laboratory. Oh what secrecy, what darkness, in which we could hardly distinguish each other. . . . How many clever men who had nothing whatsover to do with medical science received high positions under the cover of artificial secrecy. . . . False, fabricated science lived a wretched life of artificial animation. Discussions were organized in order to show to the whole world the glitter of creativity, the clash of opinions. But under this artificial light only the shabby decorations of dogmatism, ready-made reports, prompted ideas, were visible." At the end of the novel, the heroes are preoccupied with the question of whether the deplorable conditions had really been corrected or whether the Kramovites still held sway despite the appearance of improvement.

Kaverin's book is to some extent what the Party envisaged when it encouraged bold criticism, except that it goes much further than the Party wished. Instead of brushing off a few cobwebs, Kaverin made a head-on attack on conditions in science. Science is to him a most important endeavor with great potentialities for removing pain and curing and preventing disease; he is outraged by the usurpation of institutions which he considers sacred in function and unlimited in possibility by men who thwart their aims and abuse them for ends of their own.

Some of the inconsistencies of the book may perhaps be explained by the fact that the latter parts of it were written in the freer atmosphere of the thaw, whereas the earlier parts trace back to days before a substantial relaxation had set in. At any event, while chauvinistically viewed, artificial incidents (such as those cited earlier: triumphs over foreign scientists, the remarks about American profiteering in the manufacture of penicillin) occur in the book, they are contradicted by passages toward the end in which characters who clearly speak for the author condemn the same attitudes which had been favored earlier.

Clear throughout, however, are the author's extremely dark view of the extent to which the summits of Soviet scientific institutions had been penetrated by evil men (who will be considered at greater length in Chapter IV), his relief at the coming of de-Stalinization, and his reluctance to prophesy unequivocally that everything will come out satisfactorily in the end.

The date of writing and publication of a book makes a big difference in Soviet literature. Daniel Granin, we have seen, wrote the fairly conventional *Those Who Seek* between 1951 and 1954. In August 1956 he published a short story, "Personal Convictions," in *New World*, the magazine which consistently took the sharpest, freest editorial line in the course of that year. The story again deals with a technological-scientific subject, but is far more critical and outspoken than his novel had been. The increase in frankness and vehemence is a gauge of the progress of the thaw between 1954 and 1956.

Understanding of the forces working on men and of the various accommodations made by individuals is deeper here than in *Those Who Seek*. The subject of the story is mechanical engineering; the real issues, however, are human problems: the effect of power on character; the necessity for compromises with the demands of one's superiors and their consequences.

The story presents the head of a research laboratory, Minaev, who faces the criticisms of a young subordinate, Olkhovsky. The older man recognizes in the younger someone very similar to what he himself used to be: an enthusiastic, undiplomatic, truthful, tactless, crusading dissenter. In the course of the story, despite his basic sympathy and even self-identification with Olkhovsky, and although he keeps telling himself he intends to shield his subordinate from critics, Minaev finds himself maneuvered (through his own personal aspirations and the need to oblige important colleagues and superiors, to whom Olkhovsky is an uncomfortable gadfly) into collaborating with them in reprisals against him. In the end he participates in (or at least does nothing to prevent) the transfer of Olkhovsky to a position elsewhere, so as to be rid of the brave and brash engineer. But Minaev, in several introspective ruminations, gains in self-knowledge through his encounters with Olkhovsky: he realizes how, through a series of supposedly temporary compromises with authorities, he had irrevocably transformed himself from a youthful rebel into a successful, opportunistic careerist. Granin goes far beyond the criticisms he made of scientific conditions in *Those Who Seek*, as well as beyond the Party's limits of permissible criticism. The story became one of the most attacked works of recent Soviet literature.

Olkhovsky is a figure reminiscent of Molière's Alceste or of Chatsky in Griboedov's *Woe from Wit*. By implication, the society which he rightly attacks — and which eliminates him — is comparable to the corrupt Tsarist society pilloried by Griboedov. *Searches and Hopes*, Granin's own earlier novel, and other works showed powerful men opposing innovations and abusing their positions to block the worthy projects of younger men. In "Personal Convictions"

Granin represents a complete victory of the men in power and defeat of the rebellious innovator.

Moreover, the focus of the story is not really on science or technology. The spoiling of youthful aspirations, generous passions, truthfulness, and courage, not the waste of fuel in an inefficient motor, is what arouses Granin's indignation.

The shift from science as an instrument for conquering nature and advancing the material welfare of mankind to science as a bureaucracy which human beings enter with noble intentions but which transforms them into yes-men, cowards, and time-servers is quite clear in the literary techniques of the story, too: there is far more introspection and self-analysis than there is in the usual Soviet story. To Granin, science in this story is something instrumental — a means to an end. His story is primarily a tragedy of character.

"Personal Convictions" may be considered a telescoped version of Vladimir Dudintsev's *Not by Bread Alone* (*New World,* 1956), the novel which has provoked greater controversy than any other work recently published in Soviet Russia. Dudintsev's Lopatkin, a former high school teacher who is not even a full-fledged engineer, has invented a superior centrifugal pipe-casting machine. He spends the whole period of the action of the novel, seven years, in attempting to win acceptance for his machine. His main opponent is Drozdov, initially the boss of a Siberian industrial town, later a ministry official in Moscow. Many other important officials and scientists help to suppress Lopatkin's invention, for they support the academician who is responsible for the currently used pipe-casting machine (which according to Lopatkin wastes two kilograms of cast iron in every pipe it produces, besides having numerous other shortcomings in comparison with Lopatkin's model). As a result of false charges Lopatkin (like Andrei in Kaverin's *Searches and Hopes*) is sentenced by a military court to years of forced labor. Later his case is reviewed; he returns, his machine is built and accepted; yet the novel concludes with a testimonial meeting in honor of his opponent, who, together with his henchmen, is still very much in the saddle — in spite of the isolated breakthrough of Lopatkin's machine.

The novel contrasts various ways of regarding inventions; it describes the fortunes of inventors, successful and unsuccessful; it is concerned with the role to be played in Soviet life by geniuses and exceptional men, with the public need for the inventors' work, the inner nature of this work, and its similarity to the work of a poet.

Naturally such an ambitious novel encompasses issues beyond those presented by other novelists. It is not accidental that the wrath of the Party apparatus descended on Dudintsev; he courted attention by the width of the area he staked out for penetrating examination, as well as by the depth to which he reached.

An important difference between the men on Drozdov's side and those on Lopatkin's lies in their view of the nature and role of the inventor, the original scientist. The Drozdovs have little genuine esteem for him. They do not understand the importance of his work; they do not appreciate his outstanding qualities as a superior human being. They fail to value either what he is or what he can contribute. Drozdov puts this quite clearly to Lopatkin: " 'You see, Comrade Lopatkin, if I were a writer, I should write a novel about you. Because you are really a tragic figure. . . . You embody in yourself a whole epoch which has passed irrevocably into the past. You are a hero, but you work by yourself. We see you as clearly as if you were on the palm of our hand, and you do not understand us. You do not understand, for example, that we could do without your invention, even if it should be a really big invention. Yes, Comrade Lopatkin, we should not suffer a loss, because of the strict calculation and planning which assures us a steady forward movement. Let us asssume that your invention is the work of a genius. When this task which you are trying to solve appears on the agenda of the day, our construction and technical collectives will find the solution spontaneously, and this solution will be better than yours, because collective efforts always lead to the fastest and best solution to the problem. The collective has more genius than any genius. . . . There is one thing you are unable to understand. We are worker ants.' When he said this word, at the bottom of his cheerful eyes there stirred a cold monster of enmity. 'Yes — we worker ants are necessary. . . . And you, a genius, solitary, are not needed, with your giant-like idea standing on little legs.' "

In this long outburst, Drozdov articulates the normally concealed resentment of genius felt by the "worker ants." The bureaucrats, the powerful conservatives, stress group work and distrust the exceptional person. The inventor, unless he has been tied down like Gulliver by innumerable threads spun by the bureaucratic pygmies of whom Drozdov and his friends are the leaders, is dangerous and hateful to them. Drozdov says to his wife, "I do not believe in the existence of so-called 'higher natures.' Side by side with the concept of 'genius,' by necessity there existed the concept of the 'rabble.' I am a descendant of the rabble, of poverty. I have a hereditary enmity toward all those — irreplaceable — " His wife interrupts him: "What you call 'elevated nature' I call 'simple honest man' — take everything from him, turn him into a beggar, he will still give light to the people all the same."

Lopatkin's attitude toward genius is the opposite of Drozdov's. In this inventor's opinion, great value resides in the outstanding individual who can contribute something to the progress of mankind. In addition to his social, material usefulness, a genius is a grand example of humanity at its highest. Dudintsev compares the researcher to a Christ-like figure, to a poet, to a romantic hero; he is a man who "will continue to give light to the people" even when everything has been taken from him. The Soviet scientist is to Dudintsev a Prometheus, persecuted, defeated, yet holding on to his flame and helping mankind in spite of all punishment. (By implication Drozdov and the ruling powers are cast in the roles of the evil gods.)

The association of the researcher with the light-bearer is also made by reference to a line of the poet Bryusov, "We shall carry lighted lamps into the catacombs, deserts, caverns." A crushed, defeated old inventor in the novel, Busko, recollects Bryusov's words. In bemoaning the waste of talent, Dudintsev is emphasizing the importance of its "lamps" and "light."

Lopatkin's answer to Drozdov's speech on the "ants" is to interject: "One of these ants has climbed higher up on the birch tree and it thinks for everybody, decides what is useful and what is useless to the people. I am also an ant! And I don't climb up the birch, I am pulling toward the anthill a caterpillar which is ten times heavier than I am." He accuses Drozdov of setting himself up higher than the others, of usurping powers of decision-making; as for himself, he sees his own value in working for the community (the anthill) on an overwhelmingly difficult task — and instead of being helped, is hindered by his superiors.

The Drozdovs seem to Lopatkin to be "riding on the technology of yesterday. Like silkworms, they spin clothes for themselves out of their own spittle." They have established a monopoly. "They don't look forward but backward. Their aim is to maintain themselves in their armchairs and to continue to enrich themselves." On the other hand, "the discoverer of something new serves the people. The inventor is always someone who thinks differently, in any field of knowledge. Because he found a new shorter road, and rejects the old, customary one." Here again we have the belief in the double usefulness of the inventor: he is someone who is useful to his country; and he is a nonconformist, possibly a misfit, and must be recognized as such and not persecuted.

The nationalistic motivation of a Bek is rechanneled by Dudintsev from an attack against foreign enemies into an onslaught on domestic ones: those in positions of power who obstruct the inventor's road. In a discussion of his novel in Moscow, Dudintsev is reported to have explained that during the war he saw Messerschmitts outmaneuver and outfight Russian airplanes even though the Russian planes were more numerous; and yet he and others had been told by the Soviet press that their planes were the best. His own eyes disproved this. He determined that he would never again see his country's propaganda exposed in such a tragic way. He told of a second example. When there is a shiny foreign car parked in a Russian town, there is always a crowd of Russians gawking at it, admiring it. "When I see that, I begin to burn up. It seems to me that if I stand there another minute looking at it, I'll fall down and not be able to get up. It is they [the Drozdovs] who doom us to that shame," Dudintsev explained. Here the same resentment of Russian backwardness which drove Bek's characters to frenzied efforts in order to develop Soviet airplanes leads Dudintsev to a bitter attack against the bureaucrats in Soviet science — who he feels are to blame for the backwardness. He thinks his energy will be most effectively applied in negative criticism.

The finest, noblest view of the scientist is expressed by the old man, the defeated scientist, Busko, in a conversation with Lopatkin. The two men, rejected and refused help by all institutions, are eking out a living by repairing roofs of buildings. They look down at the vista of Moscow roofs; to Lopatkin, the sight suggests an analogy. There are "ground floor" people who are not dreamers, not romantics. They recognize merit only when it is acknowledged in the newspapers, when a man receives a decoration. On the other hand, there are the "discoverers of something new," who as it were have lifted themselves up to a higher floor, and from their vantage point, see which road is unsuitable and which will lead to the proper goal.

Such a discoverer of new things seems to Dudintsev's character to be a man saying to society: " 'Look, one must go this way!' He cannot create ground-floor values, because they are to him something that has been left behind. That would be just the same as making copies instead of creating great originals. [Here Dudintsev's conception of the inventor as an artist, a creator, is implied.] Forgetting himself, the second floor man hurries to grasp and turn over to the people all that he sees. He creates the greatest values and says to the ground-floor people: popularize it, multiply it. But they don't understand. They walk below in the circle of known, familiar things, and chase the old man upstairs. They work out, let us say, the process discovered by Siemens. They supply it with beautiful quotations. And in chorus they declare the discoverer to be a madman."

The scientist, the innovator, and the artist are here identified. Dudintsev accepts the term which Drozdov rejects with contempt— the inventor as an "elevated, higher" nature — and applies it to the inventor literally.

"What I have lived to see!" Lopatkin says to himself on an occasion when Drozdov had reproached him for aspiring to be an outstanding person: "A Russian sits in front of you and threatens you with the great danger — that you may become a genius in your country! One cannot be a river, one can only be a little drop. This is the opinion of the son of a country which counts great talents in tens, in big quantities. The devil with him, with me — my machine is just a small thing — but a new Lomonosov * could come to Drozdov!" The harm the Drozdovs are doing is resented on nationalistic grounds, as a rejection of Russia's past geniuses, as well as a menace to possible great geniuses of her future.

The artistic comparison is reinforced when Lopatkin goes to a concert, where "feelings of fighters and sufferers dead long ago" are revived in him. The crusader, the hero who is compared to an artist, is refreshed and inspired by the work of artists of the past in the purest medium, music. Drozdov's wife, Nadya, also sides with the true inventor — as a creative man — rather than with the "organizer" whom Drozdov prefers and holds more important: "The creative part cannot be replaced by a man of business," she tells her husband. The idealists, not the operators, not the practical men, are Dudintsev's heroes.

Dudintsev is convinced of the irreplaceability of the outstanding man capable of creativity and dedicated to it. To express his conception he resorts to images drawn from Greek mythology, Christianity (there are many biblical echoes and images in the novel), art, and Russian history (when a reference is made to what might happen if a Russian genius like Lomonosov appeared before a twentieth-century, Soviet Drozdov). He defends the great individual's uniqueness and his need to differ.

The novel about an inventor became a great manifesto for poetry, love, individuality — for intangible, spiritual, humanistic values, counterpoised to materialistic, pedestrian Drozdovism. As a result, until Pasternak displaced him, Dudintsev was the writer most in official disfavor. (In May of 1959, as we saw earlier — in Chapter I — Khrushchev went far in the direction of rehabilitating Dudinstev's reputation.)

Another writer who drew official wrath was Semen Kirsanov. His

* The great eighteenth-century scientist, poet, and thinker, one of the few near-universal men of modern history, is naturally enough frequently invoked by Soviet authors eager to advance the cause of both science and literature. Thus one of the characters in *Those Who Seek* says : "Lomonosov was the first and so far the only person able to express complex scientific ideas in good poetry. . . . There is even more poetry in Soviet science. Why shouldn't it inspire our poets?"

59

long poem "The Seven Days of the Week," which was published in *New World,* September 1956, made a most unusual use of the technological-scientific theme. This poem is a fantasy and satire which utilizes a pseudoscientific subject in order to attack general abuses; in the process it delivers several blows to bureaucratic management of inventions.

The poem deals with a doctor's effort to persuade a government ministry to manufacture new hearts to replace those of people whose own hearts have ceased to function. After drawing sketches of a new heart, he fails to obtain the necessary permissions through the five working days of the week; then on Sunday, he finds in the newspaper that Vtornikov, his enemy, is being acclaimed as a "famous innovator," and an announcement is made of an exhibition of hearts in a department store. His idea has been stolen — and misused, for he finds that stores everywhere are selling, in place of his lively heart, hearts made of rubber, and others in the shape of flasks of sweet perfumes or albums with sweet verses.

In the introduction and conclusion to the poem, hopes are expressed which are belied by the body of the work. In the first section the poet seems to be addressing himself to the "Soviet land," which he envisages as saying to the people:

> I shall not refuse requests
> Even if I have to postpone my holiday.
> I need everybody, and every dreamer
> Who is dying of thirst is dear to me.
> To me and to you, soullessness is hateful. . . .
>   Invent, think, seek.
> I shall not shut the door to you.

Yet throughout the poem the doctor is a petitioner vainly beseeching his country's rulers, until the last section, where he too expresses high hopes for the country's future.

The doctor suffers a setback at the gate of the ministry. Ironically he reads a newspaper article entitled "Looking after the Plain Soviet Citizen," when the ministry in reality does not feel any concern for the Soviet people's needs. Bureaucracy hamstrings all his efforts. On the second day, the villain Vtornikov sends the message "Don't get ahead of yourself," and fines him in order to teach him a lesson, "so that ideas would not be born / Without directives." On the third day we learn more about the nature of his concern: the new heart is to help "connections on earth," to be a means of establishing contact, to link "like the thread of wire . . . your excitement, joy, pain, love." It is to be a means of creating a renaissance of feelings — felt together, in common — of communication between people. On Thursday night, in a nightmare, he sees Vtornikov and others, as specters bearing the names Indifferent, Double-Dealer, False Witness, marching in a procession:

> In their hands they all hold the stone
> Which was in their breasts.

Then,

> Thank God, it is night,
> Not reality, but a dream.
> I wake up. I am saved.

But the waking reality is no more pleasant than the nightmare had been. On Friday, while the slogan reads, "We work together here, Party and non-Party people," he encounters a procession of the same people of whom he had dreamt. They sing an anthem:

> Such hearts are not needed for consumer goods.
> In general, new things
> Are not needed on our market.
> We need useful hearts,
> Of iron, like locks,
> Uncomplicated, convenient.
> Capable of accomplishing everything:
> Are they to blacken? They blacken.
> To value? They value.
> To fulminate against someone? They fulminate.

Only slavish hearts are wanted, hearts ready to do what they are asked — to be silent, to love, to destroy, to grow. In the corridors of ministries, on Saturday, he finds the Committee of High Feelings, the Sector of Unpostponable Matters, the Section of Humanity. But there is no response to his request:

> Take off the wax seal.
> You know that one cannot
> Forbid the beating of the heart.

61

On Sunday he finds stores selling false artificial hearts. The public is deceived:

> A lie in the shape of a heart impudently was sold
> And the public surrendered to the deception
> And a man without a heart gave to his poor girl friends
> A little heart in the shape of a copper brooch.

He is left only with the hope that the next day, another Monday, will come, and a whole new week, in which the Country will say to him and those who think like him:

> I shall distinguish the truth of the heart from falseness
> I shall not permit that desires be shut up
> In a drawer, like Cinderella in the closet.
> . . . I shall not permit that blossoms on a field in May
> Be replaced by paper blossoms.
> I shall destroy dead soullessness
> Like St. Anthony's fire or smallpox.
> Let all living hearts inside me beat,
> I am sick myself when they break.

But the comfort lies in hopes only, in imagining what may perhaps happen the next day, the next week.

Kirsanov is presenting the desire for freedom, for innovation, boldness, genuineness, for all things of the heart, through a grotesque fantasy — drawing on surgery and medicine for his humorous yet satirical purposes. He delivers thrusts at ministries undertaking to regulate subjective human emotions pompously, in offices bearing grandiose names.

In a fraction of the number of words of Dudintsev's novel, Kirsanov is making a similar analysis of Soviet society. Where Dudintsev presents a painstaking, realistic panorama of Soviet technological bureaucracy, Kirsanov dashes off a highly distorted, comic, surrealistic thumbnail sketch, with abstractions parodying morality-play names. Similarly to the author of *Not by Bread Alone*, he deplores the damming up of inventiveness, initiative, originality. Most important to him is the "petrification of the heart," the dehumanization of Russians through regimentation and emphasis on the immediately, myopically "useful."

Both Kirsanov and Granin use scientific themes as avenues of approach to an indictment of institutionalized dehumanization. It is characteristic that they, as well as Dudintsev and several other authors, as we shall see in Chapter IV, concentrate on science and technology when they wish to depict a "negative character" or villain. In scholarship, technology, even factory management, they find the most meaningful and expressive instances of evil in the form of perversion of a potentially beneficial, creative undertaking. Their preoccupation with wicked men in the laboratory and in the plant manager's office, which we shall consider later, reveals their high conception of the potentialities of the scientist and the technologist.

The unorthodox and provocative uses to which Granin, Dudintsev, and others put the science novel naturally provoked much controversy and opposition. Soviet comments made in praise and in dispraise of these works may help us to understand the frame of reference within which Soviet readers read and Soviet writers compose them.

We have already noted, in Chapter I, the debate over Dudintsev's novel at the October 22, 1956, Conference of Inventors, Efficiency Experts, and Production Innovators held in Moscow. Although the novel was attacked by some, it was stoutly defended by others. As one defender put it, "a wall stands in front of inventors" and the novelists have the duty "to give portraits of these big bureaucrats, to depict all their machinations, to show how they poison talented people. A struggle is in progress and it should be reflected in literature." The discussion dwelled on the advantages to be gained by the rank and file citizen from free exposure of the defects in science. Strictly utilitarian, economic, industrial improvements were debated, but not the moral, psychological, even political changes which Dudintsev or Granin at their boldest had in mind.

The majority seemed to be on Dudintsev's side; their position may be summed up by the statement of one: "For a long time we have failed to encourage independent interpretation of the diverse and varied phenomena of the life of society." The tenor of most comments was that unhealthy conditions existed, Stalin and Stalinism were to blame for them, and the question before society was how to revitalize the stiffened joints.

The critics hostile to Dudintsev held that he erred in suggesting that the entire state and Party apparatus was to blame for the existence of a man like Drozdov, and in making it seem as if the Drozdovs were all "top class," privileged characters, whereas in fact, the critics said, such villainous people could be found in all layers of society. It is an interesting sidelight on the supposedly classless state that some of the anti-Dudintsev spokesmen were particularly nettled by the charges against the "best people" and were virtually answering that the other, lower people were not perfect either, that conditions in general were bad.

In an article addressed to the English-speaking world and published in January 1957, a Soviet woman critic (T. Trifonova) defended writers whose science novels were under attack, mainly by asserting that their representations of conditions in Soviet science were not really so dark as people made believe. She contrasted these works with the novels of the American Mitchell Wilson. "Kaverin and Bek and Granin do not consider their theme [of the misunderstood scientist] tragic. They know that the difficulties facing inventors in our conditions arise not from the nature of the Soviet system, whose purpose is to bring about the victory of the new forces, but rather from transgressions against that system," she explained cheerfully. Moreover, the action of Dudintsev's novel "develops at the end of the forties and beginning of the fifties, when the personality cult and resultant violations of Soviet moral and legal standards were particularly marked."

Her argument hinges on her claim that "the difficulties Lopatkin encounters" are not due "to the inherent nature of life in his country." If Dudintsev regards the abuses he is describing as exceptional, untypical, and not deeply rooted in the Soviet system — and especially if he dates them as happening under Stalin, thus acquitting the present-day Soviet system — then the critic sees little which should be objected to. Mitchell Wilson, on the other hand, she declares with approval, shows that under capitalism in the United States, the "theme of the endless fight people with creative ideas have to put up" is a tragic theme because conditions of society in America are such that the desperate scientist "feels that he will never be understood."

In sharp contrast to this defense was an attack in *Party Life* (*Partiinaya Zhizn*). Directed against "Personal Convictions," the article blames Granin because "the whole story creates a mood of hopelessness and futility in the fight against evil." "Can anyone deny that our Soviet reality gives the widest opportunities to creative initiative?" asks the author, in a question which has been repeated frequently since the Soviet launchings of satellites, and then sets down the theoretical premise for his optimistic assumption that all is well in Soviet life — or at least that everything is in the process of favorable rearrangement — and hence that Granin is misrepresenting reality by being too gloomy: "In searching for acute conflicts, Granin deviated in this story from the truth of life. This latter consists in my opinion in the following. The new always arises in the fight against the old and the hardened and fights its way against many obstacles. It always has its supporters and its opponents. But one way or another, in the last analysis, the new and progressive always wins. That is precisely what Granin was unable to show. . . . Our literature should help us to live and build communism, and not sow doubts, arouse distrust of leaders, or undermine faith in Soviet man."

A more fundamental attack on recent Soviet writing about science was contained in an article by Ya. Elsberg. The author claims to be basing his argument on the same love for science which Dudintsev, Granin, and Kaverin demonstrate (but which has led them to bitterness and impatience with the impediments in the scientist's way). Elsberg charges them with having failed to do for science what seems to us to be the very heart of their accomplishment: "to give an aura of poetry to invention." He complains they have not "poeticized" the work of inventors and scientists. Elsberg even holds out to them the example of Mitchell Wilson as an author who has showed what could be done to endow scientific work with poetic glamour under "conditions of antagonistic social relations of the United States."

Elsberg refers to optimistic prophecies about what science will be

65

able to do for man. He quotes the academician D. I. Shcherbakov's remarks that "the geographer of the future will occupy himself with the active transformation of the character of separate regions, perhaps whole continents of the globe," and refers to a symposium article, "Reports from the Twenty-first Century," in which fifteen Soviet scholars tell of the wonderful prospects lying before scientists.

The brunt of Elsberg's attack is born by Nikolai Gorbunov's "The Mistake," a story in which an elderly geographer reflects about his life and decides that his whole scientific career has been a mistake and that science in Soviet Russia is "a narrow circle, amidst a chase after authority, self-protection, friendly favors and concessions, the fighting around science, a war with a bitter admixture of ambition and money interests." Elsberg is indignant that the scientist should see in his geographic studies "not a science but a collection of Ivans, Semens, monopolists and routineurs, men of indifference, devoid of principles, remote from real life and deep ideas." The story, the critic complains, is about the "degeneration and indifference of the new generation of scholars." The spirit of the story leads to a "skeptical estimate of scientific work."

An interesting contrast is drawn by Elsberg between this story and Chekhov's "The Boring Tale," in which Elsberg says the separation of the scholar from the people and life can be explained by the "exploitive structure" of society. In spite of the capitalistic Tsarist conditions under which Chekhov's professor lived, without enjoying a proper environment which would imbue him with social consciousness, he had a true love for science; he was a man of great dimensions, dedicated to what is "most beautiful and necessary in human life. . . . We feel the poetic passion of his thought."

We can easily see where the shoe pinches. Elsberg is resentful because Chekhov's portrait of a Tsarist scientist shows a man superior to his Soviet successor.

Gorbunov's hero is a scientist whose misery is really due to his personal character, rather than objective circumstances around him, Elsberg continues. At the age of fifty he is naively dreaming of returning to the life and feelings of a twenty-year-old. Incapable of fighting dogmatists and conservatives in science, he projects his own guilt on conditions in Soviet science. "Such cowardice in the struggle for a progressive science should have been ridiculed satirically, but N. Gorbunov lyrically elevated his 'hero' and made him feel seriously distressed about his 'mistake' [of choosing a scholarly career]." The author should instead have described his character as rejecting these "hysterics about the state of our science." Elsberg admits that there are people who conceal their own ignorance and ineptitude by criticizing others, "people with empty eyes and wooden faces . . . but they are having a harder time of it; every day their masks are being torn off them."

Elsberg praises Leonov's *Russian Forest,* Alexander Sharov's *The Journey Continues* (1954), and Elena Uspenskaya's *Our Summer* (1953) for successfully rendering scientific themes with the proper emotional coloring. He charges, however, that in *Not by Bread Alone* "invention lacks any poetic aura," and that Dudintsev merely centers his books on a "new universal machine for pouring cast iron pipes of any shape, up to six meters long"; the invention is regarded as a merely technical, not an artistic, phenomenon. The critic broadens his accusation to include other authors who are "unable to convey the poetry and beauty of the everyday work of Soviet man." Dudintsev, Gorbunov, and their colleagues have a "haughty, contemptuous attitude toward the everyday work of the Soviet people" (the critical essay was published under the heading "Unjustified Haughtiness"); they present it as "prosaically gray."

The Soviet successes in launching satellites have cheered official optimists, who use them as evidence that the "negative" writers distort reality. Anatoly Sofronov, an old war horse of the Stalinist line on literature, in a December 1957 issue of the *Literary Gazette* called Dudintsev, Yashin, and their likes "troubadours of negative orientation" and said that if they were right, then Russia ought to be on the technological level of the samovar, when actually she is a leading pioneer in the sciences; therefore, the picture presented by them must be false and their critics correct. This exploitation of Russian scientific advances has been adopted as the standard official line in urging writers to look to the positive side of Soviet life. The fact that it is the Granins and Dudintsevs, not Elsbergs and Sofronovs, who hold the higher and nobler views of scientific work and achievement will probably continue to go unnoticed in Soviet criticism.

These, then, are the concerns that lie at the center of any Soviet critic's consideration of his compatriots' fictional treatments of science. What is it that we of the West find worthy of note? What conclusions can we draw from our survey of Soviet fictional treatments of science? Some of them may be significant even if they appear elementary or mere confirmations of platitudes.

One such conclusion is a reaffirmation of a point made at the beginning of this chapter: that the scientist (the scholar, the technological specialist) is a very common figure in Soviet fiction; he is not in American novels. We have many books of science fiction (just as Russia has them), but we have no flourishing literature about contemporary life, seriously scrutinized, in which the scientist plays an important role.

When one surveys the scientist or scholar in Soviet writing, one is struck by the fact that many of his problems, many of the uses to which his career is put by the writer, are also treated in American fiction, where they are usually attributed not to an engineer or a forestry specialist, but to an artist (writer, painter, sculptor, musician), a politician, a lawyer, or a doctor. But not to a technological scientist. To our public and to our authors, an engineer, for example, is not a sufficiently creative or independent man. His work does not seem to engage the imagination. His problems appear dull, his professional aspirations insignificant in a broad sense.

Our engineers often complain that under actual industrial conditions it is much more difficult for them to attain professional status that for a lawyer, say, working for the same company. The lawyer, we feel, is independent. His work may make a big difference. He may save his company's hide; his clever moves may change the course of important events. Moreover, his work involves the measuring of justice, the conflict of individual wills with the will of society, and various deeply human concerns. Not so — in our view — the engineer, the specialist. He is not independent; he is given jobs to work on instead of choosing them; he is narrow, as we view him, not creative. The development of a leak-locator or a centrifugal pipe-casting machine would probably not seem to an American writer or reader to engage sufficient imaginative values, to have enough scope and human significance. It lacks glamour. The writer would be afraid of the bathos of the subject, or of just plain boredom. The theoretical or research scientist of genius would be regarded in essence as creative, but even he is not generally the protagonist of American novels.

The Soviet writer considers the changing of the curvature of the block of a tractor motor a subject of lively and deep interest, a matter of sufficient dignity to engage a fine man's deepest energies. He sees the engineer as a man of genius, an unusual man, creative and capable of contributing to the good of all mankind. He also sees him beset by temptations: to use his talent in a cheapening way (for money or without regard for social need); to buckle under a dull boss's orders and not fight until victory; to play politics and establish an empire or a monopoly of power in ministries and institutes for his own personal comfort; or to desecrate a hallowed gift by becoming discouraged and going into other fields of work. Both the opportunities and the dangers of a technological specialist's life involve the making of important decisions. They reveal his courage, social consciousness, and nationalism, and his view of his rights and obligations.

One negative finding may also be significant. In Soviet fiction we do not come across the rather common American attitude that scientists are a race apart — that the student majoring in physics, for example, is "one of *them*," a person who works very hard, knows nothing about affairs outside of his own mysterious field, and cannot be understood. In Russia scientists do not seem to be treated in the way in which some of them occasionally are in America, with a hushed reverence mixed with the sense of an unbridgeable gap between them and the rest of the population.

Scientists are regarded in Russian novels as men apart from others only so far as they are more creative and capable of contributing more. The problem is how best to employ their exceptional talents. Otherwise scientists and geniuses are considered to be, not, as they sometimes are in the United States, strange bearded men with foreign accents and retorts in their hands who are at home only in a laboratory, but men and women who belong among other people, form a normal part of the public, and are particularly necessary, since they work for the good of the society, of this generation and of the future. While scientists in Soviet novels are depicted as very useful to society, the Party men around them in the fiction of the last few years are often presented as harmful. The higher officials among them have some of the characteristics of a priesthood — a special caste of leaders who, however, in an almost Dostoevskian sense, have somehow, somewhere gone wrong. They may now be said to be working for the other side, as if they were former servants of Christ now serving the Antichrist.

But the scientist, while regarded as a benefactor of mankind, is not viewed as if he were garbed in the vestments of a priesthood; he is rather a rationalist humanitarian and a humanist. This is perhaps one of the most encouraging conclusions to be gained from the scientists in Soviet fiction. The conditions of Orwell's *1984* have not yet come about in Russia; and it appears that they never will. The values, the ideals, the hopes and aspirations as shown in the Soviet scientist are similar to the highest ones of Western culture, perhaps with only one important exception: a greater emphasis on the group, on work for the collective, than in the West.

Soviet novels display great faith in the ability of man to use his reason as a tool to conquer nature, with the aim of improving man's life on earth: to alleviate pain, cure diseases, manufacture machines, utilize natural resources. Work for the good of mankind, through the use of disciplined, trained intelligence, is worshiped. The scientists are purpose-oriented, rational men.

Interesting also is the relation of scientific work to politics. Some of the enthusiasm scientists in Soviet literature pour into scholarly work — their tremendous dedication, their love for scholarship and technology — seems to be explainable by their withdrawal from political or social action. Not necessarily in order to find safety in a neutral position, in "internal emigration," but more out of a waning of hope in political action, out of disillusionment with Party work, the nonpolitical contemporary Soviet man is taking refuge in intensive work in science.

Science instead of being a tool under the control of the Party and the political bureaucracy has become an independent value, a rival — more important than the Party which is its antithesis. The scientific work of the lonely, individual inventor is celebrated; the Party, or at least the governmental bureaucracy, is the obstacle.

The characteristic quality of Dudintsev's and his colleagues' writing is enthusiasm for inventions and for science as a poetic, creative enterprise. Soviet critics like Elsberg have missed this point — or at least they have remained silent about it in print. What they have seen (and then either supported or attacked) is Dudintsev's obvious daring in depicting the gray quality of Soviet science, the profusion of evil men of little talent in positions of power. The "poetry of science" demanded by Elsberg *is* present in Dudintsev, Leonov, Kaverin, and Granin. Elsberg will not see it because what he really wants is not poetry of science but the thinking of positive thoughts. He objects to Gorbunov's story because "neither the studies of the hero, nor his scientific work, evoke in the author of 'The Mistake' any poetic enthusiasm." When he speaks of an "aura of poetry" which the pages of Soviet fiction ought to show as emanating from Soviet scientific accomplishments, he is really asking for the sweet odor of uncritical admiration.

Thus our investigation of science in Soviet literature has led us to a paradox: those among Soviet authors who view science as a subject which lends itself to pleas for a new humanism, dignity, and freedom, and which embodies the possibilities of creation and poetry, are attacked as detractors hostile to a poetic view of Soviet technology and science.

Party critics tried to silence Dudintsev and his colleagues. Yet with the eternally recurring and ever-encouraging myopia of the censor, they have attacked the obvious subversiveness and tangible menace of the Dudintsevs — and have missed, passed by in silence, what is the most insidious, to us the most hopeful sign. Soviet critics attack these writers for "slandering reality," for describing the Soviet bureaucracy as corrupt and harmful. But they have failed to notice — or at least to mention in print — the humanistic revolt. Humanitarianism is acceptable, in the sense of science being used to advance human welfare in a collective undertaking, with men thought of as masses, crowds, or anonymous generations. But humanism, an interest in the inner well-being of the individual, rather than humanitarianism is what concerns and worries Dudintsev, Granin, and Kirsanov (and most of all, of course, Pasternak): what is happening to the individual man while the ostensibly humanitarian projects are going on?

The rebellious authors take the inventor to be the true humanist: a poet-like figure, the creative individual. They use him and his persecution to pillory the Soviet system. They expose the inner degradation of men by the system. Drozdov and Kramov are representative of the dehumanized robot — the man to whom feelings, love, and culture are things which belong only to the nineteenth century on one hand and to the remote future on the other, banished from the present, with an air of distinct superiority, as luxuries which we cannot afford right now. The humanism, the return to inner values (which is also shown in Soviet writers' treatment of love relationships) of Dudintsev and the others, is something to which the Soviet critics are blind. The passages which express the protest of the individual seem to come from the deepest place in the hearts of the authors. And it is through the creative scientist that they voice it — not through artists or politicians.

Yet one of those scientists who feel the need for reform most keenly, Dudintsev's Lopatkin, at the end of *Not by Bread Alone* seems to realize that the path to reform through technology and science alone will not reach the desired goals; that in order to achieve them, he will have to turn to "the destructive element" — immerse himself in politics. At the end of the book, he thinks he may have to abandon his directly creative yet also hermitage-like retreat for the battlefield where one can win power: to work toward reform through politics.

Characteristically Russian attitudes toward science as seen through Soviet fiction can be summarized as follows:

The worship of science is more emphatic (and perhaps more naive) than in the West.

Since similar criticism of bureaucracy, of officialdom, is very common in nineteenth-century Russian literature, the critical Soviet novelists, in this one respect at least, sometimes remind us of a Gogol, a Chekhov, a Shchedrin, or a Tolstoy.

There is particular stress on the group — on the collective.

Nationalism plays an important part in novels, either positively as love for Russia or negatively as a wish to assuage and compensate for hurt feelings of inferiority. Both aspects operate as stimuli toward scientific work. (But in the conclusion of Kaverin's novel the nationalism is shown to be an impediment.)

The career of the man of technology and science is viewed as one which is an excellent vehicle for the expression of the struggles toward creation which man must undergo both as an individual and as a member of society.

Dedication, passionate work, intellectual effort, are uniformly viewed as admirable.

Romantic, solemn feelings are regarded as quite appropriate in subjects we might consider trivial, even laughable, if taken too seriously — pipe-casting, minute improvements in techniques, for example.

The main dangers to the scientist are surrender to lethargy and defeatism — withdrawal; surrender to the evil bureaucrats above or the evil system around him; or surrender to the temptation of seeking a personal income from sources of dubious value.

The most encouraging similarity to our values lies in what some Soviet authors appeal to as the highest moral sanction of the individual's behavior. This turns out to be not the Party, not the community, as we might expect, but ultimately one's own moral convictions. The heroic engineer refuses what in Soviet Russia are socially recognized tokens of success — *dachas* (summer houses), television sets, cars, Stalin or Lenin prizes, honors — when they are accompanied by the necessity to surrender his principles, when he is asked to keep silent about which machine is really better or what should really be done to improve the new tractor. The scientist is regarded by Soviet authors of Dudintsev's persuasion as being at the peak of his moral heroism when he accepts loneliness, social disgrace, and material penalties for the sake of his innermost convictions — we should say, when he is a martyr to his own integrity.

CHAPTER III
Love **VERSUS** *Steel Production*

THE REPRESENTATIONS of love in Soviet literature have usually been closely related to the currently dominant views of the proper place of love, sex, and family life in Soviet society.

In the years immediately following 1917, family ties were somewhat loosened and relations between the sexes rendered more free by the turmoil accompanying the Revolution and the Civil War and by the influence of the ideas of the German socialist Friedrich Engels. Engels regarded the family as an exploitive institution, which would have to be abolished or fundamentally reformed in a socialistic society. Woman would be liberated from the drudgery of work in the home and put on a level of equality with the man; children would be brought up independently of their parents.

In the first years of the Soviet regime, it was natural that there should be many radical proposals to revolutionize love and family life. There were advocates of free love. Some favored the "glass of water" theory of love propounded by Madame Alexandra Kollontai, prominent Bolshevik revolutionary and later diplomat, who urged that sexual desire be satisfied as freely and unemotionally as thirst, which we quench without any fuss by simply drinking a glass of water. In her book *Love in Three Generations* Madame Kollontai wrote: "Sexual life is nothing more to me than a physiological pleasure. I change my lovers according to my mood. . . . You must have leisure to fall in love. And I have no time." Boris Pilnyak wrote in his story "The Law of the Wolf" in the 1920's: "The epoch of the October Revolution rebuilt sex morals and freed the family economically. In the human world monogamy is not a biological law." Lenin, however, opposed Madame Kollontai's "glass of water" view of love: "Of course thirst cries out to be quenched. But will a normal person under normal conditions lie down in the dirt on the road and drink from a puddle? Or even from a glass with a rim greasy from many lips? But most important of all is the social aspect. Drinking water really is an individual concern. Love involves two, and a third, a new life, may come into being. That implies an interest on the part of society, a duty to the community. . . . This liberation of love is neither new nor communistic. . . . Self-control, self-discipline, is not slavery in love any more than in anything else."

Family legislation in the twenties reflected the liberal attitudes. Marriages and divorces were easily obtained, abortions were legalized. In 1927, however, after wide discussions, a new marriage law was enacted which retreated somewhat from the theory that the family was outmoded and that free love was socially desirable. The decision to industrialize the country entailed consequences which served to strengthen the view of the family as a useful, necessary social unit. This trend was reflected in the family law of 1936 and in later measures. Family stability was now encouraged. An industrial country needed responsible, reliable citizens, who in addition to possessing various economic virtues would be good family men and women, and not the irresponsible, emotional persons associated with easy marriages, divorces, abortions, and free love. Under Stalin the trend became a veritable triumph for a Russian version of puritanism.The potentially anarchic, disruptive elements of human life were regarded with suspicion. The Party assumed the role of champion of the sanctity of motherhood and of the inviolability of the family. Love was to be carefully circumscribed. The assembly line and the combine were important, not the red rose and the love sonnet.

Literature followed suit. In the 1920's, such authors as Panteleimon Romanov (best known for his story "Without Cherry Blossoms") had concerned themselves with the emotional conflicts created in people with "old-fashioned" ideas who found themselves in a milieu deriding love as a bourgeois, sentimental prejudice. Later, Soviet novels progressively withdrew from passion and sex. This is shown amusingly in the revisions and rewritings of Soviet classics, successive editions of which were frequently altered by their authors (or editors) in order to conform to the pattern of the day. Gladkov's novel *Cement,* for example, in its original edition of 1925 presented a typical emancipated woman who would have no part of the pre-revolutionary kind of marriage. There were ardent scenes of sexual love. In later editions of *Cement,* through the thirties and forties, as the family again became hallowed and sex disreputable, the woman turned first neutral, and finally downright domestic.*

In the last years of Stalin's life, extramarital adventures and illicit loves were seldom presented in Soviet fiction, and when they were depicted, it was with vehement moral disapproval. Literary characters had to be proper and unblemished in their family lives, which in any event were overshadowed by their social and economic lives. Their primary devotion went to tractors, production quotas, and the Party. There would be little point to beginning the discussion by analyzing in detail a conventional Stalinist work, as was done in the previous chapter with depictions of scientists. The private, emotional lives of the characters would typically be undiscussed or at least unemphasized; love and sex would be carefully subordinated to the economic achievements and social commitments and concerns of the characters, with the Party always standing by as the watchdog over all behavior.

One of the signs of change after the death of Stalin was the reappearance in print and on the stage of works which flaunted the official Stalinist proprieties of love and family life.

S. Aleshin's play *Alone* (*Theater*, August 1956) presents two married couples, Varya and Pavel Nefedov, and Mariya and Sergei Platonov, who have a fifteen-year-old daughter Nina. Varya falls in love with Sergei, leaves her husband, and moves in with her father. The issue of the play, as far as plot is concerned, is whether or not Sergei will leave his wife and daughter and live with Varya. At first he decides against it, but later he changes his mind and determines to do so.

The bare outline of the action hardly seems sensational or even

* An illuminating as well as entertaining account of the changes dictated by ideological considerations of the Party line is given in Maurice Friedberg, "New Editions of Soviet *Belles-Lettres,*" *American Slavic and East European Review,* 14:72–88 (February 1954).

interesting. The main concern of the dramatist, however, lies in the discussions and presentations of situations giving substance to the skeletal plot. Aleshin shows the characters struggling with their personal problems: a husband unhappy over leaving his wife and daughter; a father forced to watch his daughter leave her husband after falling in love with a married man; a wife miserable because her husband leaves her and her daughter and because she dreads the prospect of years of loneliness ahead of her.

Through most of the play, the emphasis is on the problems of the two persons in love with each other, Varya and Sergei — on the motives drawing them into divorce and a new marriage and on those which cause them to dread wrecking their present families. In the last scene, attention shifts to what is suggested by the title of the play, *Alone* (in Russian, *Odna*; with the feminine ending it means literally "a woman alone"), the fate of an abandoned, divorced woman. Aleshin prepares for this denouement by planting in the play two other women, Lida and Margarita, one of them a divorcée who has taken refuge in loose living and debauchery as an escape from her loneliness, the other a three-times divorced, also lonely woman. Lida and Margarita supply perspective to the subject of a woman finding herself "alone" after years of marriage; they show that what may happen to Mariya is not a unique fate.

Aleshin's concentration on the thoughts and feelings of the individuals involved is remarkable. He averts his eyes from possible broader social consequences of the situations he describes. The writers of the 1930's, 1940's, and early 1950's would have stressed the considerations owed to Party interests and to public morality. The example to be provided for others, the duty to the Party, the necessity to uphold the new "firm Soviet family" — these would have been emphasized. It would have been shown that only scoundrels divorce their wives or husbands and fall in love with persons other than their lawful spouses. Aleshin repudiates this social and narrowly moralistic bias. As if to underline that his sole concern is with the effects marital and romantic involvements have on the happiness of the individual, he introduces a Party man who represents the conventional, anti-divorce, hypocritical, socially minded attitudes, only to expose him and refute his arguments. Andrei Kravtsov, a fifty-year-old member of the Party committee, tries to interfere with Sergei. "You have a family," he tells him. "Can't you do it in some other way? Mariya is hurt, Nefedov is hurt, the little daughter is hurt. (Whispers.) Couldn't it be done in a quieter way?" This Party spokesman tries to persuade Sergei to give up his infatuation, if possible, for the sake of his family and his reputation, or, if he cannot, to carry on with his sweetheart secretly, instead of openly: "If you don't feel pity for anybody else, at least have respect for public opinion. Keep quiet about it. Everybody understands — all sorts of things happen. Everybody is not an angel. You are kicking against the goad. . . . They will take your Party membership card away from you."

Sergei easily disposes of Kravtsov's dishonest arguments: "I earned my Party membership card on the front. I can defend it. The Party does not need me to lie. The Party needs me to be honest, to work honestly, to have a family life based on love. That is what the Party needs. To have me always be honest. Yes. We have only one life, and he who lies deceives himself and the Party both."

Aleshin arranges the circumstances of the dispute so that the choice to be made is between the honesty of Sergei and the duplicity of Kravtsov. Aleshin does not confront Sergei with what would have been a stronger and more interesting opponent than Kravtsov, a Party man urging with the strongest arguments which could be mustered that family loyalty instead of personal attachment should prevail.

The case for following the call of love is argued by Varya. Pavel had not been a bad husband to her; she had loved him, but he gave in to her in everything and did not insist on her having children. He agreed with her too much. "At times a woman needs to be told 'No,'" Varya declares. "To have things explained, proved, to be told 'I want to have a baby by you.' Understand? A woman needs to be begged, to be asked to give birth to a baby! Pavel agreed to everything. He could take no for an answer. Now I know what it is to want a baby. I want a baby from Sergei. I want to be a mother. I want the baby to be his. Let it cry, soil diapers, everything. Only he must look like him. And he wants that from me." Her father asks: "You are going to have a baby, Varenka?" "No. As long as he is living with his family, no. Oh, father, how beautiful it is to feel a man's will close to oneself. . . . Everything about him interests me. Every detail. Why he combs his hair like this and not like that. Why he doesn't wear rubbers. These facts are of tremendous importance. . . . I now breathe differently. . . . I speak with people as if I had some special knowledge."

Her father, however, finds it difficult to accept the fact that she has left her first husband and intends to marry another man. He blames himself for having brought her up badly — he was a widower and thinks the absence of motherly care is responsible for his daughter's misadventures: "Somehow there was something I was incapable of imparting to her. *Mea culpa* — my fault. . . . How casually they deal with each other. And this is a serious woman, your daughter," he says to himself in his solitary reflections. "And what about the ones who are not serious? Abortions, men, their own husbands, other people's, it makes no difference to them."

When Sergei comes to see him, looks at a portrait of his late wife, and says, "This must be Varya's mother?" the father answers sarcastically, "Yes, her mother, my wife. A rare combination nowadays, don't you think?" But Sergei, after fending off the father's remarks, launches, before this unlikely audience, into his own eulogy of love, a counterpart to the one which Varya had just delivered to her father: "It always seemed to me that they wrote a great deal about love. Now I understand they write too little about it. When someone's every little hair, every little scrap of paper on which she wrote even a word, become sacred objects. . . . And now that I have lived to feel that happiness, am I to strangle it?"

The father argues for the opposite view much more effectively than the Party man had done:

Vasily: You think you have lived to feel happiness? I think your wife and Nefedov are of a different mind. You know what? I am a surgeon. All my life I have cut up living people. I have become accustomed to their being in pain. But if I cut them up in order to cause them pain, and not in order to stop it, I should be not a surgeon but a butcher.

Sergei: It is myself I am cutting up.

Vasily: That it not true. You are not the one who is in greatest pain. It would be a different matter if your life at home had been sheer misery. There is no need to go on living in misery. But it was not misery.

Sergei: No, it was not.

Vasily: It was not. So that means that after love is gone, there still remains duty.

Sergei: It does not seem to you that what you call duty — is the same as misery? It would be curious to see what decision you would make, if you were in my place.

Vasily: Well, you know —

Sergei: (brusquely) I know. You are about to say that you would never find yourself in my place. Or something else equally pharisaically nutritious: with vitamins in it, but without taste. A lie. It may be that you are such a lucky man that you met right away the woman for whom the love in your heart was waiting. Few people are so lucky. More often — a man lives all his life without finding real love. Simply never meets anybody. Or meets her late, and becomes a coward. How will things be with my wife? What will people say?

Alone is a problem play dealing with love and family questions so important to the individuals concerned that in contrast to them the needs of society and the vested interests of the Party are insignificant; the Party's view has shrunk to a despicable argument presented by Kravtsov only to be contradicted and forgotten. The Party, as the official spokesman for society, is not even honored by having a decent, strong case presented on its behalf.

The mere fact that a writer is acknowledging the great power of love by devoting a play to its effects on several individuals would hardly be surprising in the West. We are likely to take such attitudes for granted. Public and personal claims conflicted in the loves of Virgil's Aeneas and Dido and Shakespeare's Antony and Cleopatra. We are not likely to be surprised by a twentieth-century French, English, or American novelist who assumes that love is a great thing and very important to the individual man and woman. Why should we pay so much attention to Aleshin's play, then? His *Alone* is remarkable for the very same reasons which would make it commonplace in the West. It is an index of the gap between Soviet Russia and the Western world that in Russia it should be a noteworthy, most startling fact — not missed by Aleshin's critics or supporters — that his play approaches familial and amatory problems from the point of view of the individual's private concerns. To the completely politicalized and economized Stalinist man Aleshin opposes men and women whose private lives still possess considerable emotional substance and who heed the claims of their loves.

The conflict between group opinion — opposed to any disturbance of the family — and the emotions of the individuals involved is also the issue in a controversial poem by an Armenian poet, Paruyir Sevak, "A Difficult Conversation," translated into Russian by Evgeny Evtushenko in the June 1956 *New World*. In this poem a young man is in love with a married woman. The "group" takes up the matter:

> The meeting lasted
> for some five hours.
> They considered everything.
> They came up with the decision:
> I must
> "interrupt relations" with you.
> What sort of a name — is that —
> "relations"!
> They explained to me ardently and clearly
> That one must avoid
> Family dramas.

The poet's attitude is one of dismay over the insensitivity, lack of understanding, and arrogance of the "group" which, after a bureaucratic conference, gives him directions, couched in clichés and jargon, concerning his private emotional life. The Soviet Armenian poet implies in a few lines what Aleshin expounded in many scenes of his play: that he doubts the ability of any conference, any collective organization, to understand fully what is happening between two individuals who are in love, that he believes any facile recommendation or order passed down by a social watchdog organization (in most cases, the Party) will be a ridiculous distortion of the emotional situation, and that he disputes its right to pass judgment on a love affair. The irony of tone in the line "they considered everything," as well as the reference to the length of the meeting, suggests the poet's bitterness and outrage at the violence done to private emotions.

81

Viktor Nekrasov's *Home Town* (1954) also delves into the subjective feelings of individuals, concentrating primarily on love and eschewing consideration of Party or other "group" interference. The first half of the book is one of the greatest accomplishments of Soviet prose fiction since the end of the war. The last portion unfortunately falls below that level, becoming a conventional Soviet novel, with its typed villain, a social message, and a stock scene of acrimonious controversy at a conference. But the early part of Nekrasov's novel is a story of wartime soldiers' return to civilian life which bears comparison with the best Western works dealing with similar subjects.

Two wounded men — Nikolai, formerly a captain, who has a disabled right arm, and Sergei, a flier who lost a leg — return to Kiev in the last stages of the war when the Russian armies are advancing from Poland into Germany. Sergei has become a manipulator in the black market, peddling slippers throughout liberated Ukraine; Nikolai, still staying at an army hospital, is looking for his wife. He wanders from one destroyed building to another, until he is referred to the apartment where his wife now lives. She is not home. He waits for her until it becomes clear to him that she is now living with another man, and he leaves. Later they do meet.

Most of the characters in the book, the principal and the minor figures, appear dazed. There is very little conversation, curiosity, or surprise. Everybody acts as if he has just survived an earthquake and dug himself out of the rubble. The whole city is barely in contact with life. Men walk around like machines, without much emotional reaction to anything and without interest in other people. Nekrasov presents an image of relations between men and women who after the upheaval of the war and the disappearance of normality have become fatalistic, casual, devoid of feeling or soul-searching.

Nikolai's wife Shura had remained in the city under the German occupation while he was in the army. The young man with whom she is now living was a soldier in the Russian Army which liberated Kiev. The circumstances through which Shura — who knew nothing of the whereabouts of her husband or even whether he was still alive — came to be living with another man are described by the author as inevitable events natural under emergency conditions. The flavor of the passage can best be conveyed by an extensive quotation:

She remained alone, altogether alone in an empty apartment. In the daytime she sat in the attic while the Germans were going from apartment to apartment, at night she went downstairs.

On the night of November 6 there was continual shooting in the streets. She spent the entire night in the attic. Through the dormer window she could see the whole town burning. In the morning she went downstairs into the apartment. There were soldiers in it, our soldiers.

Can Nikolai understand what it means to see our men after two and a half years? After the Germans had been as far as Stalingrad and all day the radio shouted that the Soviet Army was almost entirely annihilated? Can he understand that? She looked at these soldiers — dirty, overgrown, smelling through and through of cheap tobacco and sweat, and they looked most beautiful to her.

One of them was wounded — a very young lieutenant, some kind of a commanding officer of theirs. He could not be carried elsewhere and so he lay there, on the only bed, and she nursed him. The hospitals were overcrowded, people were lying on the floor. His outfit moved forward, he remained in her place.

The neighbors — new ones who came after the liberation of the town — began to gossip almost from the first day. In talking with her they never called him anything but "your man." "A letter came for your man. Your man again splashed water all around the washbasin."

Both his legs were shot through. This was obviously very painful, but he did not moan. He only clenched his teeth and stared at the ceiling. When the soldiers were leaving, many of them cried. They liked their lieutenant and behind his back called him Fedyusha. He was younger than the youngest of his men — only nineteen and looked like even less than that. He had down on his upper lip and no beard at all. . . .

They took him into the hospital. She brought him food. . . pitiful rolls and sour cream, which he liked very much. . . . They demobilized him. . . . He had nowhere to live. His family, father and mother, lived somewhere near Riga — his father before the war worked in the VEF plant — but the Germans were still there. She did what she thought anybody in her place would have done — he had lived there for almost three months already and in any case the neighbors called him "your man."

And that happened which could not help but happen when two young people live under the same roof.

Was it love? On Fedya's part, it was. It is even possible that this was his first true love, the first love of a man who went straight from the classroom into the whirlpool of war and in this whirlpool came across a woman who showed affection for him. And on Shura's part? Obviously, it was also love. But this was some other kind of love, quite special, born of compassion for this very young, seriously wounded man, the first man with a red star on his military cap whom she saw after two and a half years of occupation.

In that way, at least, poor Shura, all going to pieces, herself not knowing what was going on, explained it to herself. All these years she had thought only about Nikolai. At night, closing her eyes, she lay and thought about him. . . . She did not believe he was dead, she waited for him. . . . Can Nikolai understand that? Will he want to? Understand her loneliness, her longing. She waited for Nikolai, but he was not there. She waited for letters, and they also were not there. She understood that the longer Fedya lived with her, the more complicated her position would become. But she could do nothing with herself, she feared loneliness, above all she feared loneliness. She waited for Nikolai.

And now he had come. And she did not tell him anything. She did not find the courage in herself to be the first to speak of it.

Nekrasov's characters are bewildered and overpowered by the military and political events which engulfed them. A curious automatism has taken over the guidance of their physical and emotional movements. They are hardly able to be clear in their own minds about what they wish to do and what they feel; they go on acting — appearing to be taking decisions — when actually they are only going through the outward forms of action. They cannot communicate. Nikolai and Shura, when they finally meet, speak of trivialities — and part again, seemingly impassively, although afterwards both of them are overcome by emotion and regret. Yet when they were talking to each other, they were unable to speak of anything personal and deep. It was as if a gigantic frost had frozen their emotions.

Shura's young soldier soon leaves her, without complicated explanations. He sees that her husband has come back to town and feels he is no longer really wanted. Matter-of-factly, he picks himself up and returns to Riga, now liberated from the Germans. Shura lives with Nikolai again. A little later Nikolai goes back to study at the university, leaves her, and lives in a dormitory. Then — and this is her final change of mate in the novel — she lives with Nikolai's wartime friend, Sergei, who is more like her than the other two men. Each of these switches is carried out simply, without elaborate explanations, in an almost animal way. Each person feels, as it were instinctively, what he should do or wants to do — and does it. The surface, not the depths of the person, is involved.

Another kind of relationship obtains between Nikolai and Valya, whom he eventually marries, the daughter of a hospital librarian. She had been in the army, too; she can talk to Nikolai in soldier slang. Her mother is horrified by her coarse expressions. But she is one person with whom Nikolai can communicate, although only within very narrow limits: he feels that she, unlike the others, knows what army life has been. They share the same recollections and reactions to civilian life. Particularly their military idiom links them. They are two veterans who understand each other. At the same time their reliance on the former military service which they have in common prevents them from finding a deeper understanding; he cannot regard her as a woman. For a long time, she is a buddy, not a replacement for Shura. Only after much readjustment does she become his wife.

It is a matter of discussion among Soviet readers and critics whether Nekrasov has been influenced in his techniques of portraying human emotions by American writers (in particular Hemingway) and by twentieth-century French novelists. Whether or not any such links can be traced between his work and that of Western authors, the very fact that this question should have come up points to the exceptional position of Nekrasov among Soviet authors. *Home Town* struck its readers as unusual, strange. It is a novel which succeeds in conveying, through understatement and an almost behavioristically restrained depiction of outward acts, the feeling of private experience which its main characters undergo. It stands out through its psychological penetration and its attention to human feelings, particularly congealed, inarticulate feelings.

In Turgenev, Chekhov, and Tolstoy we find occasions on which men and women are incapable of expressing their emotions — the scene in *Anna Karenina,* for example, in which a man and a woman go mushroom-picking and contrary to everyone's expectations prove unable to become engaged to each other, and the similar situation in *The Cherry Orchard,* between Lopakhin and Varya. In *Home Town,* it seems as if the paralysis has become general. It takes a shock, a jolt, or physical contact, to release a flow or even a trickle of emotions or words. In Nekrasov this seems due to the effects of war experiences. On the other hand, it has become remarkably simple, easy, and common for a man to move in with a woman, and to move out again.

Soviet novels frequently contain scenes in which two persons find themselves unable to express what they strongly feel and wish to communicate. This situation is especially characteristic of lovers, of persons about to confess their love for each other. Ilya Ehrenburg's *The Thaw* expresses this inhibition particularly well in a scene between the engineer Sokolovsky and the doctor Vera Scherer: "Evgeny does not know what to talk about. There just is no subject for conversation and he cannot think of one now. . . . Before, when I came, we all talked, sometimes there were pauses, but we talked, and now it doesn't work. Something changed. . . . Vera also feels it. How long can one sit in silence?" Sokolovsky then tries to start a conversation, but the attempt is forced and awkward, and it fails. It does more harm than good. The obvious artificiality of his effort merely intensifies the tension in the air.

To experience difficulty in establishing emotional contact with another human being, particularly in expressing one's attachment, is of course not peculiarly Soviet or even Russian, but universally human. In Soviet literature, however, it appears slightly more accentuated than normally. It seems to be connected with the general atrophy of the individual's emotional self-expression, caused by concentration on the economic, political, social, and industrially productive side of life.

Ilya Ehrenburg, in *The Thaw,* linked the overcoming of the emotional freeze with the general theme of "the thaw":

He waits for her patiently, standing by the window. Outside the window there is agitation. The winter was finally shaken. On the street the snow has melted, everything is flowing. Only out there, in the garden, there is a little snow. The little window is open and one does not feel it. Pity that the big window is puttied shut, one can't open it. Through the little window, voices are heard.

Everything suddenly became alive and loud.

Funny! Vera will come right away and I am not even thinking what I'll say to her. I'll say nothing to her. Or I'll say: "Vera, the thaw is here."

Evidently the unthawing of emotions was to Ehrenburg part of the process of liberalization after Stalin's death — a desirable human consequence of the general change.

In Nikolai Pogodin's play *Petrarch's Sonnet* (published in *Literary Moscow,* Vol. II, 1956), love not merely plays an important part, but is the very subject of the play. Pogodin has written a thesis play contrasting two ways of looking at love: the narrow, inhuman, even antihuman, and the individualistic, human, poetic.

The action takes place in a Siberian town. Dmitri Sukhodolov, a middle-aged married man, is working on a big construction project on the river where the town is situated. He meets a young girl from Leningrad, Maya, who is temporarily assigned to the library of the Siberian city to do a research project on the characteristics of the Soviet reader. Sukhodolov and Maya fall in love, a pure, idealistic, Petrarchan love. They correspond. Maya's roommate, Klara, a puritanical, unimaginative, fanatical Party girl, denounces their platonic love to a senior Party official, Pavel, steals and copies the letters Sukhodolov had sent to Maya, and brings them to Pavel. Sukhodolov's wife, Kseniya, a coarse, unpleasant, selfish woman, is also told about what she takes to be Sukhodolov's "affair." Unable to conceive that he could be writing love letters to a girl and addressing her in poetic terms without having an affair with her, she jumps to the conclusion that Maya is his mistress and makes a horrible scene in Maya's room. The play ends with a vindication of Sukhodolov's honor — before the Party and his friends — but in the final scene he and Maya have a talk immediately before her departure for Leningrad, with clear suggestions that this is not the last meeting between them, their relationship in the future may continue, and their love be consummated.

Pogodin uses the rather meager plot to present important ideas on love. The play is a manifesto of a man's right to his personal feelings, to love — Petrarchan, platonic, or other — as something inherently his, belonging to all human beings, residing beyond the area in which the Party may legitimately interfere.

The keynote of the play is struck in an encounter between characters identified merely as "The Girl in Blue" and "The Girl in Gray." In an argument about music, the Girl in Blue says, "It is impossible to go anywhere with you. You think only about one thing, what mobilizes you and what demobilizes you." The other girl says, "Music affects me negatively. It demobilizes me," and continues, "What is art for? In order to mobilize."

This utilitarian view of the function of art is contradicted by Maya, who asserts a few minutes later: "Music is a pure feeling." From this aesthetic, nonpolitical understanding of music, in Pogodin's view, it is only one step toward a similarly tolerant, easygoing view of love as an emotion which is each person's own private business. When Klara comes to Pavel in order to denounce Sukhodolov and brings his letters, Pavel says to her: "Why must you turn them over to anybody? Sukhodolov is writing not to me, not to you, but to a girl. This girl, I presume, keeps his letters. So let them stay with that girl." When he leaves, Klara says about him sarcastically: "He is being a great big liberal!"

Sukhodolov argues that love is primarily a man's private business. It is noteworthy that the author has Sukhodolov refer to Dostoevsky as his authority, despite the fact that Dostoevsky's views of life — often religious, antirevolutionary, mystical — are usually considered reactionary by Soviet writers, even by those who praise his literary art. Sukhodolov says to Pavel, "One Russian classic says that not only you and I, but even a father talking to his son must not speak about his relations with a woman, even if those relations are the purest. Why can't we follow laws set by that great moral view?" Pavel asks: "Who said that?" Sukhodolov answers: "Dostoevsky."

Sukhodolov sums up his point of view — the opposite of Klara's, the same as Pavel's — succinctly: "There are things which one cannot tell the Party. If it were a political matter, cut my head off. . . .

I'll give my whole soul, my life to the Party. . . . But there can be intimate sides to a man's life into which he will not initiate anybody. He simply is not obliged to; there is no such rule."

This view of the inviolacy and privacy of love is extended by Sukhodolov so that it applies to an area far broader than relations between men and women. It leads to a wish for gentler, kinder treatment of all people: "I consider class hatred a holy, noble feeling. But nowadays we do not in reality have any hostile classes. Whom shall we hate? There exist a few scoundrels, some scum, thieves. . . . They deserve perhaps contempt, at times even compassion. I am speaking about great hate. Whom in my country should I hate? Maybe it is time to learn to love."

It is clear that those on the opposed side, whose spokesman is Klara, are also not concerned exclusively with love but with the proper place of human emotions in general. According to them feelings are all to be controlled and supervised by the Party. "If you thought about everything on your own, made all decisions on your own, you would go crazy," Klara says. "One can't live without regulations. Emotions also fall within definite limits." Pavel contradicts her: "We are working out a new Communist morality, and that is a lengthy, painful, even tragic job. . . . The program of our Party gives tremendous scope to independent thought. . . . Are we, members of the Party, who occupy responsible positions, obliged to have no poetry, no tremor of the soul, no song? You, a young woman who is spreading cultural knowledge among us, saw in [Sukhodolov's] tiny holiday of human feeling nothing but cause to drag a member of the Party to an accounting."

Pavel does not believe that the coming of the Soviet era has swept away all human tragedies and emotional involvements. Whereas Sukhodolov invokes Dostoevsky as an authority, Pavel refers to another prerevolutionary, non-Communist authority: "Tolstoy was right. There have been and there shall be tragedies despite world-shaking events and revolutionary upheavals."

The positive exhortations of Pavel, Maya, and Sukhodolov are balanced by their attacks against persons representing the opposite point of view, who are uniformly described as *meshchane*, bourgeois, or petty middle-class people. It is striking how frequently recent Russian books have made *meshchane* their target. The word is difficult to translate; in the nineteenth century, it was applied to smug, petty, materialistic, dull, uninspired people. In those days they were usually described as belonging to what we might call middle-class groups. Gorky entitled one of his plays *Meshchane* (*Petty Bourgeois,* or *Smug Citizens*). It was the revolutionaries who prided themselves on opposing the *meshchane* characteristics, wherever and in whomever found. It is ironic that forty years after the Revolution, *meshchanstvo* should not have disappeared from Russia, but is now being exposed as still flourishing, not among the survivors of the pre-Revolutionary aristocracy or bourgeoisie, not among elements hostile to the Soviet regime, but on the contrary among the solidly entrenched Soviet officials, the prosperous Soviet wives, the enthusiastic Party members.

Sukhodolov's wife Kseniya personifies the most vulgar characteristics of *meshchanstvo*. She uses vile language to attack her husband after a friend suggests to her that he is in love with another woman. "Tell me, honey, what kind of a sweetie pie did you pick yourself up?" she says. "What's she like? How much does she charge? Where does she sleep nights?" Later she comments, "This isn't just some kind of an affair; affairs one could forgive; this is Love with a capital L. . . . Even if there is nothing to it in fact, if it is nothing but fantasies and dreams, that makes no difference. . . . Let him be careful about his dreams. Now that we have solid Soviet families, he won't get any enjoyment out of these dreams. I'll show him his Laura! . . . . I'll show him his poetry!"

Pavel crosses swords with Dononov, a self-satisfied, prim official ever ready to condemn others: "Oh come on, you with your bourgeois virtues!" he tells him. Dononov objects: "So a solid family is to you something bourgeois?" Pavel answers, "The family is not bourgeois . . . but your family virtues, elevated into a social cult, that is bourgeois. In that way we'll get to the point where we shall be debating over women who committed adultery or had illegitimate children. . . . A new world is being born, in pain," he sums up. "I repeat the simple truth that it is being born. But we must fight the bourgeois. They want to see even communism turned into a bourgeois paradise. They want to have peace and quiet, to be well fed, to have no thoughts."

Pogodin shows that the "bourgeois" attitudes and strict Party-direction of all life caused a great deal of harm in the past and must be eliminated if the Russian people is to enjoy a decent future. Dononov, the dogmatist, tells Pavel that he is "accustomed to judge with definiteness." Pavel answers: "Because of that definiteness, people often were put in jail. Now we can't find out which of them deserved it and which did not." He calls Dononov a *meshchanin,* tells him that the world consists of a great many more shadings than the two he is familiar with, black and white, and reaffirms a version of Soviet humanism: "In my opinion, the most beautiful thing in life is man — and not every kind of man. . . . When I run across a man, our contemporary Soviet man, who has tremendous spiritual beauty, I find life more joyous for myself. For a man free of capitalism, new, endowed with . . . integrity and spiritual beauty, is to me a kind of a joy. In him I see the future of the world, of communism. Communism does not consist of things, but of people."

Sukhodolov concludes the play: "It is joyful to have more future ahead of one than past behind one." Pogodin's main feelings expressed in the play spring from his relief at the passing of Stalinism. He is looking back romantically to the "heroic phase of the Revolution" and the early days of Soviet Russia. Soviet history since then he regards as a dark period, the abuses of which are to be corrected where possible, and forgotten where they cannot be corrected. All one's efforts are to be directed toward the future — a freer, more individualistic, humanistic future. Starting with the theme of love and its place in Soviet society, he extends the range of his polemic to embrace the broad area of inner life, emotional and artistic, presented as autonomous, outside the jurisdiction of the Party.

Galina Nikolaeva's long novel *A Battle on the Way* (*October,* March, May, and July 1957) combines several lines of plot, each of which alone would suffice to fill the average Soviet novel. There are two main centers of interest: one is urban — a tractor factory, in which Dmitri Bakhirev, a production engineer, tries to remove flaws in the current tractor model and through his honesty comes into conflict with the director Valgan, the villain of the piece; and the other is rural — a collective farm. The two locales are linked not only through some of the workers in the factory who come from the region where the farm is situated, but also through one of the faulty tractors, which throws its flywheel on that particular farm. Bakhirev consequently visits the site and becomes acquainted with some of the local farming problems, which are parallel to the industrial and bureaucratic difficulties he faces. In each of the two rings of Nikolaeva's circus, there is a similar struggle between old-line Stalinists and new, honest, efficient progressives, who are liberal and democratic in their view of the party and the bureaucracy's functions. In addition to the two geographical focal points, there are the stories of the lives of Dmitri Bakhirev and Tina Karamysh, carried through in detail from their childhood up to the present.

Love is only one of several subjects of this extraordinarily complex novel, which interweaves in an intricate pattern technology and personal lives, farm and factory concerns, politics and sex. Yet love is dealt with in such detail and presented with so much variety that the novel is a richer storehouse of descriptions and analyses of contemporary Soviet love relationships than any of the other books we are examining.

The first extraordinary image of love we find in the novel forms part of the account of Dmitri's childhood. American visitors to Russia and sociologists studying Soviet family life often speculate about the psychological consequences of the crowded living conditions in a Russian apartment, their effect on sex life and on the outlook of children sleeping in the same room with their parents and several brothers and sisters. Soviet writers usually pass by this topic in silence. In *A Battle on the Way* we find one of the very rare literary descriptions of a scene which must be repeated in one form or another in many Soviet homes, accompanied by an indication of the psychological consequences of the lack of privacy.

Dmitri grows up in a crowded apartment. His father is a drunkard who alternately abuses and caresses his wife. Eventually his wife, too, takes to drink. Nikolaeva describes their home life as follows: "In good moments, his father sat down on the bed alongside his mother, stroked her face and shoulders, and, delighting in her beauty, said, 'My good one, my beautiful one, best one of all.' But if his mother as much as stirred, he shouted, 'Don't move!' For many years these words stayed in Dmitri's ears, the tender 'mine, mine,' and the loud 'Don't move.' The parents' love was sometimes more horrible than the parents' fights. The son saw it all. Father, mother, and other drunken couples sometimes rolled on the floor, right then and there, in the small room. From childhood on, he was filled with loathing for that repulsive thing they called love. When he grew up, he avoided girls. What the girls were inviting in their subconscious girlish play arose before him in its naked and coarse form." Later he moves away and eventually overcomes his aversion for women. He marries Katya, the daughter of his landlord, who cooks fritters for him, is kind to him, and whom he misses when she goes to the country for a holiday — so he goes after her, brings her back, and marries her. As in Nekrasov, we find here the accident of living together in the same apartment presented as a common and natural cause of marriage.

Like most courtships in Soviet novels, Dmitri and Katya's is remarkably unemotional, matter-of-fact, sudden. Very little is said about love or "romance": the young people become used to each other's presence, grow fond of each other, find they miss each other — the young man proposes, the parents mumble a few words, and the couple registers its marriage. Everything moves very quickly and with little expenditure of words or show of feelings. Fending off loneliness seems to be the main motive pushing the young people into marriage.

Dmitri's counterpart, Tina Karamysh, the chief female figure in the novel, goes through two marriages and a love affair with Dmitri. When she is twenty-three, she marries Ignaty, an older man, a fine and noble high official in the Party. She lives the life of a Soviet aristocratic damsel, studying watercolor and oil painting, English and German. She is a very devoted, considerate, thoughtful wife, but her serene dilettantism is accompanied by sexual and emotional im-

93

maturity. Although her husband "at first lived in the hope that with the maturity of her body, maturity of feeling would also come . . . year after year the difference between them widened."

Galina Nikolaeva presents a detailed and psychologically rich account of the personal relations between the couple — mostly from the point of view of the two individuals concerned, not from the emphatically social point of view of Stalinist writers. She traces the progress of the artificial, protected married life of Tina. Ignaty — feeling insecure because he senses the precariousness of their relationship — attempts to protect her from contact with anything unpleasant and coarse, anything which might take her away from him. A friend tells him: "Are you making the girl into a trout which lives only in pure, high mountain streams? In life such streams are few and far between!"

Ironically, Tina matures and her love for her husband grows warm only immediately before he is taken away from her. A Jewish friend of theirs, Professor Geizman, is arrested on false charges at the height of the Stalinist anti-Semitic campaign, which Galina Nikolaeva describes with terrifying frankness. Ignaty defends Geizman courageously and is also arrested. Shortly afterwards Tina is informed that he has died. Only when Tina realized the danger hanging over Ignaty's head did they enjoy a brief, belated flare-up of mutual love — broken off by his arrest and death.

Ignaty, the Party man, tried to induce Tina to prefer the Party to her personal feelings in the conflict which he knew would inevitably occur in her mind after his unjust arrest. He told her: "It is better not to believe in me. Don't believe in yourself. Believe in the Party. Believe in that which the best people of two centuries have put into it. Without that faith, one cannot live."

But his words are in vain. The shock of his arrest hurls Tina into a marginal existence — rooming with a blackmarket operator, doubting everything, all her emotions paralyzed after her disillusionment with the Party for which she had lived previously.

After a period of gradual emergence from her paralyzing depression, she becomes acquainted with Volodya, the son of her landlady. Volodya grows to love her with a dog-like devotion, without telling her about his feelings for her. He even takes to sleeping on the floor outside the door of her room, without her knowledge. The author explains that Tina's eventual marriage to Volodya is due to her wish to find a shelter against the cold, inhospitable life into which she had been cast after losing Ignaty: "She loved both of them [mother and son] and their little house. What was there, beyond the low white walls, Tina could not and did not try to understand. But in that tiny piece of the world fenced off by those walls, everything was clear, warm, and clean. Here one could move and breathe, rest one's heart, become oneself. Tina wanted to fence herself in behind these walls and live in her own little, good world, where all was intelligible and close to the soul, where nothing of the incomprehensible inhumanity of the human world tormented the mind and heart."

Volodya is a little vague and colorless. Their marriage does not withstand the shock of another love affair. Tina works in the same factory as Dmitri, they fall desperately in love, and Galina Nikolaeva takes us in great detail through the successive stages of their affair: the long months during which each of them tries to keep his feelings secret from the other; the growth of physical love between them; their long love affair, both idealistic and sordid, in a dirty, broken-down room which the stepfather of one of Dmitri's Siberian army comrades, recently dead of wartime wounds, allows him to use for their meetings; the step-by-step destruction of the beauty of their love through its enforced furtiveness and sordidness; its discovery by Dmitri's wife.

Galina Nikolaeva refrains from adding an artificial happy ending. The reader trembles as he reads lest through some novelistic trick she should jettison the surplus husband and wife and conclude her novel in a happy, married clinch of Dmitri and Tina, and he is pleased when she maintains her integrity to the end. It is clear that Galina Nikolaeva understands and approves of Tina's and Dmitri's feelings. She suggests they had been looking for each other all their lives; their legal spouses were not their "true loves." It is equally clear that the author feels a divorce would be in order, except that Dmitri has children, and, it is repeated several times, he is not the kind of man who abandons his children. Upon being discovered by his wife — who has turned out to be an unpleasantly selfish, squirrel-brained, dull, mediocre woman — under circumstances which cause a scandal throughout the town, he returns to his wife and family, and Tina leaves the town alone. (Her husband moves in with another woman who had loved him all along.) Dmitri is a martyr to his work and family obligations, but not so much as Tina, who after her terrible experience of the murder of her first husband by Stalin's police finds herself once again alone, about to start the search for a new career and personal life.

The author's account of all the love affairs and marriages, in number and variety rivaling those of Cozzens' *By Love Possessed,* is remarkable for its scrupulous honesty. She never falsifies either her heroes or the role played by the Party in their lives. She attributes to love and to other emotions of which love is representative an importance greatly exceeding that admitted by Stalinist writers. She devotes scores of pages to painstaking analyses of the thoughts and feelings of various characters about each other. Tina's relations with Ignaty, Volodya, and particularly Dmitri are neither extraneous trifles nor personal luxuries to be easily and willingly sacrificed on the altar of Party needs and demands, as many a Stalinist author would have presented them. Galina Nikolaeva views the loves of Dmitri and Tina as deep, complex, and of cardinal importance in their lives.

Galina Nikolaeva manages to mingle the public interest and the personal in about equal proportions, both in the space she allows them in her novel and in the weighting she gives them in the motives and thoughts of her characters. She admits honestly that at times conflicts do occur between social interests (or Party wishes) and personal desires; that at times, even, the Party is wrong and the individual justified (as in the arrest of Tina's husband, Ignaty). She is aware that the claims of society may serve as pretexts to persecute people, to force them into dishonesty (for example, into supporting the granting of a prize to a tractor model not deserving such an honor) or even into terrible crimes (the arrest and execution of Jews and their defenders). Public interest engages Galina Nikolaeva's warm sympathies only when it is directly linked to personal, individual interest: the building of more efficient tractors; removing faults in a tractor block or flywheel suspension; improving techniques of collective farming. Such issues as these, involving improvements of productive methods in a country with a shortage economy, become the legitimate, passionate goals of her heroes, of men like Dmitri Bakhirev.

The Party is safely restored to respect and to control, at the end of her novel. But on the way to it, in numerous battles, the author shows that the Party men are often dangerously wrong and she does not hesitate to raise fundamental issues (What is happiness? Which course of behavior is good and which evil?) without immediately turning to answers provided by the Party. She presents human individuals searching laboriously for their own answers.

Tina and Dmitri show a nineteenth-century Russian eagerness to discuss big, eternal questions, with the hope that the demands made by Communists principles will somehow turn out to be identical with those of their own personal integrity. They are capable of swift transitions from universal ethics to party sanctions and from them to personal love:

"It is important to know 'what is good,' as Mayakovsky wrote. What do you think is good? What is happiness?"

"Happiness is faithfulness and truthfulness to oneself. I mean — faithfulness to Communist principles. And — "

"And?"

"For happiness, one other thing is important — it is necessary to find a true echo in someone else, someone close." He looked into her eyes and drew her to himself.

Galina Nikolaeva traces the fine filaments connecting the two lovers and the nuances of the progression of their relations. Without moralistically condemning them for their adultery, she reveals the corrupting influence on them of the need to hide and their inability to live together openly. With honesty equal to Tolstoy's, but with a kindness perhaps greater than Tolstoy showed toward Anna Karenina, Galina Nikolaeva writes: "Like flies, they beat about in the cobweb of their own feelings. The great thing which at first brought them close to each other was gone. In the factory, now, unwillingly, they avoided each other, and in their little room there was hardly enough time for their hasty caresses. Love, squeezed between four walls, became choked, bent over, blind — yet continued to grow."

Dmitri blames the languishing of their love on the "times" and on material circumstances of Soviet life: "Socialistic times do not lend themselves to adultery. Take capitalism — everything is at your disposal, for money: hotels, private houses, other people, even other people's papers. All can be bought. But try to fix yourself up in our times — apartments are communal; without the house leader and a dwelling permit, there is nothing doing. In hotels they ask you for official authorizations and passports."

She answers more seriously: "Light romances of the type described by Maupassant are not necessary or interesting to us. They are too cheap for us. We've grown accustomed to greater inner values. . . . Our life has been filled with so much significance! And with big feeling. . . . Big things are always dangerous when they can't develop naturally. . . . If you close off the natural course of a large river, it can become destructive. . . . Big love needs big space to breathe in. . . . Love in the backyard is not for us."

Their illicit relations are not condemned by the author for being illicit, or antisocial, or contrary to the Party directives on family life (although a Party man who suspects the love affair warns Dmitri by saying to him significantly, "A family creates confidence and sympathy. . . . Our people like the family spirit"). The author shows the affair to be destructive because it affords no possibility of a natural growth and affects adversely the individuals directly concerned. (Dmitri will not leave his children and Tina cannot bear children since her miscarriage after her husband was arrested and shot as an enemy of the people.)

The hardships, the injustices, the human suffering which Galina Nikolaeva describes so frankly, whether they be Tina's or others, she ultimately accepts, but never excuses. A Party secretary is her spokesman toward the end of the novel when he says at a meeting at which the villains of the story are exposed and removed: "Some regard these victims [of industrialization which was necessary in order to defeat Germany in the war] as a grievous and temporary necessity, which must be stopped as quickly as possible. Others see in it something natural and regular, about which it is not worthwhile to think and about which it is harmful to talk. We hold the first view."

Galina Nikolaeva's book is a strong plea for the speediest elimination of all deeds of inhumanity by man to man. The subjective values of human love are the bastion of her humanism. This is a novel of as great variety as power. In its original version, it contains almost pastoral scenes describing the childhood of Tina, uninhibited accounts of love, moving renderings of inner dilemmas facing the characters, and frank analyses of Beria's terror and its effect on individuals.

Characteristic of the stricter atmosphere of Soviet literary life late in 1958 are the changes which Galina Nikolaeva made in her novel when she revised it for publication that year in book form. (The novel then became one of the prominent candidates for the Lenin Prize and during 1959 received much favorable official publicity, which would hardly have been forthcoming for the earlier magazine version discussed in this chapter.)

The most drastic transformation concerns Tina Karamysh's husband Ignaty: he disappears entirely from the book and some of the incidents in which he participated are transferred to Tina's father. This metamorphosis of husband into father evidently resulted from objections to what a Soviet critic, G. Lenoble, called Tina's excessive "previous experience." If Tina is to introduce the theme of love into the novel (in her affair with Dmitri), Lenoble explained, it is somewhat inappropriate that she has already been married twice, each time without knowing true love. The same Soviet critic also objected to several other points in the novel which have been brought out in this chapter, such as the accidental nature of Tina's meeting with Volodya and the lack of clarity, the "muddiness" (as he called it) in her relations with her older husband, Ignaty. In the book version of late 1958, all these faults are set straight; most of the passages quoted above have disappeared. Tina is made more proper. She is allowed to remain maidenly, even virginal. Ignaty vanishes as a husband and his brave defense of Professor Geizman is attributed to Tina's father, who is presented as a stalwart Communist. After her father's arrest (blamed on Beria) Tina is not expelled from the

Komsomol, because Volodya intervenes on her behalf and makes it possible for her to keep her membership. Thus she is saved both from excessive disillusionment with the Party and from having to be thrown into Volodya's arms almost accidentally, through the circumstances of her living quarters. He is now a young man whom she had previously known in school and in the Komsomol, he wins her sympathies by defending her against expulsion when her father is arrested, and the sympathies grow into love. Everything is decent, heroic, and Party-spirited. Moreover, some of the outspoken love scenes of the magazine version have disappeared from the book, after having been objected to as "naturalistic" by Soviet critics.

Various forms of love are connected with one of the main issues of Vladimir Dudintsev's *Not by Bread Alone* — the question What is the nature of a true human being? Lopatkin, the hero, is one example of an outstanding person; another is Nadya, at first the wife of the villain Drozdov, later the mistress and eventually wife of Lopatkin. The dehumanized men are Drozdov himself and his associates.

By tracing the emotional involvements of Nadya, we can follow both what Dudintsev thinks of love and what he thinks of the characters he is describing. He uses love — and the lack of love — as a yardstick with which to measure the human qualities of his characters.

Nadya is Drozdov's second wife; he is an older man. Public opinion has it that he left his first wife to marry the younger, taller, prettier Nadya, but the truth is that his first wife had left him. Nadya married him because he seemed to her to be the rough, energetic, pioneering type exemplified by the heroes of Jack London: "She loved the novels of Jack London and it seemed to her that Drozdov was somehow similar to the gold prospector in the novel *Burning Daylight*. She even came here, to Siberia, with the secret hope of meeting such a hero, a man capable of welding together the strength of thousands of men — capricious, cold-blooded, quick to take offense, exacting — of laborers and technicians." When she met Drozdov, her Siberian reincarnation of Jack London's heroes, he was still married. His first wife for a time refused to give him a divorce;

Nadya became his "unofficial wife." Drozdov's explanation of why his first marriage failed is significant: "She left, but I was to blame," he says. "I was carried away by work, and she needed a personal life." This last simple sentence is the crux of most recent Soviet writing: the need for a "personal life" in conflict with the demands of industry and the Party.

It soon becomes clear that Nadya, too, wants a personal life which Drozdov is as incapable of giving to her as he was to his first wife. He persuades her to reject the view of life which she had been taught since she was a child and to accept his "roughly simplified outlook on life." He is concentrating all his energies on his work; his main interest and duty are the building of the "economic foundations" of Soviet life; all else, all emotional, personal satisfaction, will have to wait. In a later chapter we shall look at Drozdov's views in more detail; suffice it to say here that Nadya becomes profoundly dissatisfied with Drozdov's conception of a full life. She feels herself to be starved for something she considers vital; she is living an emotionally incomplete life. All that she cherishes, Drozdov relegates to the remote past — or future — as "nineteenth-century things," not today's.

To the Soviet novelist of recent years, men appear more prone than women to become absorbed in "socialistic construction," in what we might call a mania for work, while women resist this tendency and incline to other values. Nadya is repelled by the robot-like Drozdov. She leaves him and falls in love with Lopatkin, whom she supports heroically in his days of hardship. She waits for him while he is serving his term in a work camp, and it is with him, Drozdov's antithesis, that she is joined at the close of the novel, with a man who dares to be an individualist, a warm, human person who loves music and thinks of life and his work in terms of the arts.

An interesting analogy to the relationship between Nadya and Drozdov is presented in an earlier novel, Vera Panova's *Kruzhilikha* (*Banner*, November and December 1947). (Panova is also the author of two very interesting works published later, during the interval of freedom, *The Seasons of the Year* and *Seryozha*. But *Kruzhilikha*, written under Stalin, is used here since it supplies a comparison —

101

both of similarities and differences — with the works written after
1954.) In this novel of factory life, written under Stalin — and at the
time of publication severely criticized for some of its attitudes — we
find a character who is a prototype of Drozdov, a factory director
named Listopad. Listopad feels the same urgency in his industrial
work as Drozdov; he works the same long hours; he gives equally
little thought to his home life. There are two important differences,
however, which may be due to the novel's being published under
Stalin, rather than in the post-Stalinist era: Listopad is reformed
and ends as an admirable character; and his wife, Klavdia, unlike
Nadya, does not leave him but continues to live with him, confining
her expression of dissatisfaction to her secret shorthand diary. She
dies in childbirth. Listopad has all the shorthand papers he discovers
among her possessions transcribed. The diary contains passages elo-
quently condemning, from a wife's point of view, the Listopad-
Drozdov manner of living:

If, for instance, I graduate from the Institute and they send me
to work in some other town (this will not happen, but let us suppose
so) — would he transfer there also? Never. Because here is the work
to which he is attached. And I — I come last of all. If I die, he will
get along without me.

I thought that when people were in love, they were always
together. But we are apart. Of course, he is very busy, I understand it, I respect his job, how could one not respect it. But if only
he were sorry, you understand — if only he were sorry that we are
apart! Our short little meetings are enough for him. Very, very
seldom does he tell me anything about himself. Once he told me a
little about when he was a boy. He does not ask me what happened
at the Institute, how the exams are coming along. I had some terrible
trouble — I lost my Young Communist League membership card.
How much running around I had to do! And he only made jokes
about it.

Some of Klavdia's complaints might seem trivial, but she considers
them due to something deeply rooted in her husband. The novel
presents Listopad as a type commonly thrown up by the Soviet
industrial system. Klavdia writes in her diary:

He is simply like that . . . he never says, you are dearer to
me than anything else in the world. He will not tell our son that,

either. . . . For a moment, between work and sleep, he will notice
our son and think to himself, Oh, yes, and he will pay attention to
him a little.

Yesterday I started crying in his presence. He became frightened
and asked me what was the matter. I told him — If you at least spent
one day with me, only one day! He somehow became perplexed,
then he stroked me and said, "All right, tomorrow I'll come home
early." And really, today he came home at two (not at night, but in
the afternoon). I was happy, ran to put on a new dressing gown,
and heard him saying over the telephone, "Ryabukhin, stop by my
place, there's something I want to see you about." Right after lunch,
Ryabukhin came. They talked business the whole time. Ryabukhin
didn't leave until six. Sasha came into the bedroom, lay down on
the bed and said — "Well, here we are, just the two of us; would you
like to go to the theater?" I saw that he was falling asleep. The last
words he was saying already half asleep. I sat there for a long time
and watched him sleep. How terribly, terribly I did *not* love him
then! I said deliberately loudly: "Why did you lie to me, and told
me that you love me? I should have been happy without you and
I am unhappy with you." He didn't hear; he slept soundly. I asked
still louder: "Why *am* I sitting here, next to you? Did they save
my life [during the blockade of Leningrad] so that I should sit here
like this with you?" And I began to put questions to him one after
another. "Why did you marry me? Who are you to me? What am I
to do?" I asked him so loud that I frightened myself, yet he went on
sleeping. . . . I am sorry if I am asking for more than I have
coming to me, but I cannot live without happiness.

Anna, the woman who deciphers and types the diary, shows her
approval of Klavdia's sentiments and her antipathy for Listopad by
thinking to herself, as she decides to turn over to him only the
transcripts of Klavdia's lecture notes and other impersonal material,
"At best he will only have time to look through these transcripts.
And hardly even that."

Klavdia's diary is striking to an American reader, first of all,
because it describes a situation widely known in our country. We
are all too familiar (in everyday life and in such novels as *Man in
the Gray Flannel Suit*) with the man who is completely absorbed
in his business and has no reserves of interest or vitality left for his
personal life after a strenuous day or week in his office, working
for an enterprise which demands and receives from him every ounce

of his energy. Secondly, Klavdia's comments demonstrate the success Soviet planners have had, since 1928, in changing the psychology of their people. Once they embarked on a program of industrialization, it became necessary to produce a "new man," dedicated to his economic function and endowed with the virtues necessary for efficient operation of a growing, modern technological empire. The individuals now most in demand were thrifty, sober, ambitious, eager to add to their technical skills and qualifications, hard-driving, and efficient. Such a catalogue of modern industrial virtues leaves little room for the personal realm of life — the arts, family concerns, personal emotions, passion, love, extramarital or, for that matter, marital relations. Listopad and Drozdov are products of this new school; they are one hundred per cent Soviet. Panova, in Stalinist days, eager to arrive at some cheerful, rosy, optimistic solution, succeeded in the end in converting her dehumanized figure into a positive character; but Dudintsev did not. In *Not by Bread Alone*, Drozdov stands condemned, both as an industrial executive and as an individual. The author shows a clear preference for the completely human Nadya and Lopatkin, who are capable of "nineteenth-century" love.

In the treatment of love and family life, Soviet fiction presents a running commentary on social conditions and Party policies from 1917 to the present. In the 1920's, authors such as Romanov and Pilnyak realized, sometimes with fascination, sometimes with horror, that the task of remaking human society would entail forging anew the patterns of fundamental human relationships. In their works they presented case studies of individuals caught up in a society in turmoil, a melting pot not of nationalities but of conflicting attitudes toward basic human problems.

After the thirties, particularly during the last years of Stalin's life, the social implications of marriage and love were stressed to the point of overshadowing, almost eliminating, the personal. The ideal of love expressed in literature became similar to the "new primness" proclaimed in Russian life by the Party. Free love, far from being regarded as a sign of Revolutionary emancipation, was stigmatized as harmful to the progress of the country. Industrialization left little room for love — free, extramarital, or marital.

After Stalin's death, the liberation of writers in subject matter and in attitude toward it led to an improvement of the literary fare offered to Soviet readers. There can be little doubt that the novels of Nekrasov and Nikolaeva, for example, are far more interesting reading than the Stalinist books turned out in the late 1940's. Real human concerns, treated not in a routine, mechanical, formulistic way, but in the author's own, genuine, personal manner, can be found in the pages of the new literature. One can speak of literary creation in this connection instead of mere production: one can sense the individual, original mind of the writer at work, giving its picture of concrete, individual situations. As a result the imaginations of Soviet readers ceased to be so starved as they had been before 1954.

In the years 1954–1957, there was a new resurgence of the Russian thirst for emotional satisfactions derived from sources other than overfulfilling one's production quota of cast iron. Love, in various forms, treated as important for the individual and described with far greater frankness than had been possible in Soviet literature for two decades, made its comeback. It returned as one of the main expressions of a new humanism, closely connected with similar attitudes expressed through discussions of science and human evil.

Original, individual creation, achieved by man sometimes working against the majority, against the group, was celebrated in some of the books on science. Love and family life as private concerns of the individuals, feelings as something with which the Party has little to do, but which are of primary importance to the hero and the heroine — these form a second private reserve or, to change the image, an island of private life for which the authors struggle. There is then a connection between the authors' strivings in the field of science and in the field of love. We shall see in the next chapter how the villains in their books tended to become men who failed to understand or who opposed the seeking of individuality, privacy, subjectivity.

CHAPTER IV

Versions of a SOVIET INFERNO

SOVIET WRITERS and critics frequently discuss the nature of the hero of their novels and plays. In fact the hero in Soviet literature is one of the favorite topics of Soviet criticism. Comments on what his opposite, the villain, ought to be, are less numerous. At times Soviet spokesmen — as we shall see — have disapproved of the portraits of villains presented in Soviet books, but they have seldom been considerate or rash enough to accompany their remarks with explanations of what kind of villain would have met with their approval. It is easier to be positive about the positive characters, negative about the negative, than the other way around.

If literature is to serve as a tool for shaping the ideas of the reader, if writers, in Stalin's phrase, are "engineers of the human soul," then the positive example to be set before him — the human model of conduct to emulate — will be the first consideration. Yet to us the Soviet literary hero often reveals little beyond the official hagiology of the Party. Most of the heroes are very similar. Pavlik, the hero of Maxim Gorky's prerevolutionary *The Mother* (1907), is one of their ancestors; Pavel Korchagin, of Nikolai Ostrovsky's *How the Steel Is Tempered* (1934), is his direct Soviet descendant. Their numerous brothers and cousins share a great number of traits. Most of them are plaster saints who differ only in the degree to which they are unconvincing. They are all either devoted Communists and revolutionaries or quick converts to a Marxist view of life who thereafter devote their lives to furthering the Communist cause, with only occasional backsliding and temporary surrender to temptations.*

* A splendid recent study of the exemplary characters of nineteenth- as well as twentieth-century Russian literature is Rufus W. Mathewson, Jr., *The*

Historically, the positive heroes can be traced back to nineteenth-century Russian efforts to create a literary character who would be a man of action, self-assertive, determined, goal-conscious, in contrast to the characters who had come to dominate the pages of Russian novels — the so-called "superfluous men," the semi-Byronic, tired, ineffectual heroes of Lermontov, Goncharov, Turgenev, and others, characters who knew what they were against and what was wrong with the society of their day, but found no means of applying their energies in practical work toward reform and the establishment of a better society in the future. From Nikolai Chernyshevsky's novel *What Is to Be Done?* (1864) on, Russian authors tried to remedy this defect and to supply adequate heroic characters.

Theoretically, the positive heroes of Soviet days can be linked to the voluntarist tradition within the Russian revolutionary movements and within Marxism — those wings in both groups which refused to rely upon a "spontaneous" development of conditions, upon an automatic, gradual evolution of social and economic circumstances without the deliberate interference of man, and instead urged the formation of a closely knit organization which would exert human will power in trying to bring about those conditions which they considered desirable, that state of society which they considered ideal or at least an improvement on the existing state of affairs. Such men of course were likely to be decisive, unhesitating, efficient, hard, unyielding men of action. In an early novel of the Soviet period, *The Rout* (1927) by Alexander Fadeev, for instance, the hero is a leader of Bolshevik guerrillas who drives his men with single-minded determination. Nikolai Ostrovsky's novel mentioned above, *How the Steel Is Tempered,* became one of the most popular of all such didactic works during the Stalinist period. Pavel Korchagin — like the author of the book himself — was a devoted young Communist who, prevented by illness from working physically toward the building of socialism, determined to do at least that which he could — propagandize through writing. Both the literary character and the young novelist, who died in 1936, the victim of his long illness, became

---

Positive Hero in Russian Literature (New York: Columbia University Press, 1958).

adulated examples set before Russian youth. A whole gallery of very similar (one is tempted to call them nauseatingly similar) heroes has been turned out by Soviet authors.

The villains, on the other hand, present more variety to our view. They are infinitely more interesting and more enlightening than the heroes. In some periods, it is true, villains almost disappeared from Soviet literature or were limited to pre-Revolutionary characters or citizens of foreign, capitalist countries. This happened in the "Zhdanov period" after 1946 when the Soviet authorities began to be concerned about the depiction of Soviet reality in literature, much as a worrisome mother might be about her daughter's somewhat bespattered reputation. A critical presentation of a character who happened to be an agricultural specialist would call forth telegrams of protest from organizations of Russian agricultural experts, proclaiming the virtues of the men in their field and attacking the author as an enemy of their entire profession. Gradually writers realized that an attack on any individual could be interpreted as an attack on the whole group to which he belonged, in fact on the whole country, and taken as evidence of a negative attitude toward Soviet Russia and communism — a rather dangerous predicament for a Russian writer. Unfavorable portrayals of Soviet citizens became very rare.

The greatest harm was done in the field of drama. A poem can easily exist without a negative portrait, a novel under some difficulty; but a play with only admirable characters is likely to be soporific. It can hardly contain any action, any conflict: a group of characters composed exclusively of wonderful persons will be likely to live in a state of perfect harmony; there will be no controversy which is not soon solved in a spirit of friendship and love. The spectators will go to sleep, if they bother to come to the theater in the first place. This is exactly what happened. Frightened dramatists turned out dull playlets full of perfect Soviet heroes and heroines. Audiences groaned and dwindled. One critic of the drama, perhaps with tongue in cheek, even advanced the theory that in Soviet drama, as distinguished from capitalist or Tsarist drama, absence of conflict or "conflictlessness" was natural and logical, since Soviet life no longer produced harmful people or social "contradictions." There could be no basic disagreements; hence drama faithfully representing Soviet life would be devoid of conflicts. To find that Soviet plays lack conflicts, then, was in this critic's opinion nothing to be marveled at. It was a matter for self-congratulation rather than concern.

Such was the situation at the death of Stalin. Villains were restricted to a few categories: foreign spies and enemies of Russia, such as American journalists attacking Soviet Russia; characters predating 1917; and Soviet citizens who in fact were the products of pre-1917 conditions and hence considered "survivals of capitalism," rather than outgrowths of the Soviet system for whom that system might be held accountable.

After the death of Stalin, one of the main ways in which Soviet writers reacted to their expanded freedom was by creating a series of "villains" or "negative characters" such as they would not have dared to include in a work intended for publication in Stalinist Russia. This gallery of villains to be found in Soviet fiction between 1954 and 1957 supplies us with various insights not to be gleaned from other sources.

The nature of villains in Soviet literature between 1954 and 1957 is important for several reasons. They show us clearly what the writers consider dangerous and harmful; they give us an insight into the author's ethics, negative as well as positive; they illustrate what is desirable as well as what is reprehensible. Not only openly admitted, conscious fears are revealed through them but unconscious, secret worries, dislikes, and resentments. The characteristics attributed by writers to their negative creations also afford us a view into their political and social likes and dislikes. Again the villain may be more useful to us than his positive counterpart. In any event he is an essential supplement to the hero, the other side of the coin. Thus the evil bureaucrat or scientist is an indispensable adjunct to the exemplary scientist whom we considered in an earlier chapter.

Writers, moreover, find it easier to make a literary success of a scoundrel than a saint. Even a mediocre craftsman may create an interesting criminal and corrupt person; it takes a Shakespeare, a Tolstoy, or a Dostoevsky to create a convincing and engrossing positive hero. Great artists are rare in all periods. The average writers, who, as in all other times, abounded even in Soviet Russia in the years 1954-1957, produced dull and monotonous positive characters, but they managed to endow their villains with more life and vigor.

Negative characters are more likely to display a complex personality with a number of traits, which usually are a guarantee of variety. Even when variety is lacking, the villains' dominant weakness may suffice to sustain interest in them. Very likely they will be men of passion. Moreover, in Soviet Russia, as in all countries with a closely supervised literature, a villain has two other advantages. First, he may be a means of saying what otherwise would expose the author to the charge of hostility toward the government; the author can disassociate himself by claiming that anything put into the mouth of a villain is meant not to be accepted but refuted. Secondly, the thoughts, deeds, and words of a villain may cause the writer to divulge views of which he may not be entirely aware. Many an obscure fact about Soviet life may turn up in the course of an account of the career of fictional scoundrels; unwittingly the author creating a character may open a secret compartment of his heart, revealing a buried wish or frustration. Villains, more than heroes, have the strange magnetic property of attracting to themselves not fully acknowledged thoughts, feelings, and facts. Examining what Soviet authors do *not* like, what they hate, fear, attack, may give us a deeper understanding of what they want, love, demand, than their direct, explicit wishes and eulogies.

In our Dantesque task of classifying the numerous Soviet negative characters, let us begin by taking a look at the type closest to the old-fashioned Stalinist villains: a man who is intimately connected with foreign or pre-1917 ways of life and thought, consciously anti-Soviet, the truth of whose life — if fully known — would obviously and incontrovertibly condemn him as a hostile element, a deliberate avowed enemy of Soviet Russia.

The very incarnation of the type — but an exceptionally capably conceived and executed character — is Gratsiansky in Leonid Leonov's *Russian Forest*. Alexander Gratsiansky, the main antagonist of the novel's positive hero, Ivan Vikhrov, illustrates the characteristics of an all-black, old-fashioned, Stalinist villain. At the same time, however, he is a very interesting and colorful figure. To some extent he even pushes into the background Vikhrov, who is meant to be the admirable central figure. Vikhrov seems rather stupid, hesitant, easy to fool; Gratsiansky, for all his Satanic characteristics — or perhaps because of them — is never dull.

Gratsiansky's evil-doing is both public and private. His long career of inflicting injuries on Russia, however, outshines his personal failings and the private wrongs he does to his enemies. He is a forestry specialist who is a parasite on the body politic of Soviet forestry. He chooses Vikhrov as his victim. He has not himself written any major work on the science of forestry, but waits for every successive book of his rival Vikhrov and then writes a devastating review of it. His hostile reviews have become famous among the men in the field. No one expresses his view of a new work by Vikhrov until after Gratsiansky's comment has appeared in print. Gratsiansky's attacks are most influential; they are also very skillful and eloquent. Leonov particularly praises their style, the implication being that their superficial brilliance makes up for the emptiness of their content. (Soviet authors frequently associate superficial dazzling qualities of speech or writing with the villain, sober, awkward, plain talk with the positive hero.) This self-designated watchdog professes to disagree with Vikhrov on basic principles of forest use. As we have seen in Chapter II, Gratsiansky advocates carefree, unlimited exploitation of Soviet forests, based on a belief in their inexhaustibility. He calls Vikhrov's plan for careful, limited felling, accompanied by systematic reforestation, a reflection of capitalistic views and a timid procedure harmful to the expansion of Socialistic economy.

The eventual defeat of Gratsiansky is handled very effectively by Leonov. It occurs after Vikhrov, convinced that it is hopeless for him to continue to struggle, comes to say that he is going to give up. "You have won," he tells Gratsiansky. "Not as far as my theoretical views are concerned — I am opposed as before to American migratory exploitation of forests with complete felling of woods — in other words, as before, I favor rational, planned, constant utilization. But you defeated me in something else — I took up a job beyond my strength." Vikhrov's surrender ironically frightens Gratsiansky whose whole position is predicated on parasitism. He needs someone, a Vikhrov, to continue making positive suggestions, so that he can fasten on to them and advance his own career by destructive rebuttals. If Vikhrov withdraws from the battlefield, Gratsiansky will have to take over — and everyone will see, once his ideas are put to the test of practice, that he has been wrong and has nothing positive to contribute. He will then be judged by his deeds, by the quantity of wood available annually to the industry under his direction, not by the sound effects of his words.

Gratsiansky begins to hesitate. Vikhrov perceives that "this man is afraid above all else of being left alone with the Russian forest." Gratsiansky's full unmasking follows quickly. Behind the front of a devoted Soviet scholar lay hidden a long, dark personal history. Leonov reveals Gratsiansky's past as well as his nefarious present by flashbacks and reminiscences of his youth in the period before 1917, interwoven with the narrative set in the first two years of World War II. Gratsiansky was the son of a professor of theology — a wealthy boy, then, with a suspect family background. The darkest blot in his past is revealed by Leonov last of all, close to the end of the novel. Associated with the fringes of a revolutionary group of students, Gratsiansky fell victim to Emma, a notorious woman employed by the Tsarist secret police. Supposing her to be the wife of Chandvetsky, a secret police officer, Gratsiansky fell in love with her and even revealed to her the name and activities of a revolutionary, Valery Krainov, who was then arrested by the Tsarist police. Gratsiansky, infatuated with Emma, wanted her to divorce or leave Chandvetsky — only to discover that she was not his wife but an agent of the police. He found himself in the power of the police because of what he had revealed to Emma and because the police could ruin his standing with all his friends if they made it known that Gratsiansky was the person responsible for Valery's arrest. After the Revolution, Gratsiansky succeeded in removing incriminating documents from the archives, and most witnesses of his actions were dead by 1941. Still, he lives in perpetual terror of revelation — with justification, for Chandvetsky, living abroad, re-emerges in Gratsiansky's life through a foreign botanist who visits him. Thus Gratsiansky turns out to be a villain connected both with prerevolutionary, Tsarist, secret police activities and more tangentially with counterrevolutionary, foreign intrigues against the Soviet Union.

Leonov rounds out Gratsiansky's villainy still further. He attributes to him a variety of other views associated in Soviet Russia with prerevolutionary, decadent thinking. His philosophy of history is similar to Tolstoy's. With weary agnosticism, he expounds to Polya Vikhrova, the hero's daughter, the view that human reason is incapable of fathoming the numerous factors which move history. He says that every period has its own conception of the causes that are important in history; the future may make discoveries unsuspected in the present; wars seem eternal to him; peace is a brief interruption of the series of wars. With gloomy fatalism he expounds his view of history as a not very meaningful procession of wars, from Darius, Xerxes, and Timur to Napoleon and Hitler. By implication, he is contradicting Soviet Marxism — with its confidence that it understands the main moving springs of history and is able to manipulate them. Gratsiansky is presented as a very seductive spokesman for the *fin-de-siècle*, decadent, degenerate, bourgeois, anti-Marxist view of history and war.

If Gratsiansky's historical disquisition is somewhat Tolstoyan, then his views of suicide are reminiscent of those of some of Dostoevsky's characters. Vikhrov picks up a little notebook on Gratsiansky's desk, which contains a collection of notes on suicide. It is an anthology of classical and Western literature on the subject accompanied by Gratsiansky's comments. (Here as elsewhere, Gratsiansky's propensity to collect historical analogues and to refer to classical, medieval, and Western learning is presented by Leonov as a somewhat suspect, non-Soviet trait.) "The death wish is God's anguish for the failure of his creation" and "THIS [suicide] is the only thing in which man surpasses God, who could not annihilate himself even if he wished to" are typical of Gratsiansky's entries in the notebook. Leonov is using them to show Gratsiansky as an inwardly corroded man incapable of life, sunk into self-destructive ruminations paralleling his destructive moves against Vikhrov, the representative of the healthy, constructive, Soviet tendencies.

Gratsiansky in fact ends by committing suicide — drowning himself in a hole dug in a frozen river. Leonov makes a derogatory comment on Gratsiansky even in speaking of the suicide. He calls this "old-fashioned method" of taking one's life rather surprising for the "well-fed and pampered" Gratsiansky, since it would be "extremely cold."

When one lists the characteristics of Gratsiansky it is a little difficult to see wherein his fascination lies, yet it is palpably present. He sounds, in summary, like an impossibly complete villain — destructive, connected with non-Soviet, prerevolutionary Russia, son of a professor of theology — a negative character of astonishingly complete negativity. Yet as he lives in Leonov's novel, he is convincing and fascinating. Leonov has him speak in a strange, puzzling, mysterious manner: long sentences, profusions of references to history, vague insinuations, meandering thoughts. There is something uncanny in his style as well as in the content of what he is saying — something hard to put one's finger on, an elusive, elastic quality — dark threats and innuendoes which he withdraws and covers up as soon as a direct question is put to him about them. He is a dark, diabolic character also in his own mysterious fear — the hints of secrets in his own past — which are finally explained as the history of his involvement with Emma and her secret police employers.

Leonov's Gratsiansky, then, is a particularly Satanic, Dostoevskian, and artistically successful villain, despite the fact that in his main traits he corresponds to the Stalinist prescription for a negative character. He is original, curiosity-provoking, shudder-inducing — one of Leonov's best creations.

Yet for all his personal traits which set him apart as an individual, Gratsiansky traces back, in the fundamental qualities which make him a negative character, to the traditional, old-fashioned villain of Soviet literature. He is a survival of prerevolutionary ways of thinking and an alien, inimical element in Soviet life. Such, after all, had been the usual villains in Russian literature since 1917. A characteristic work of the thirties, Afinogenev's play *Fear*, with its black-and-white division of characters and attitudes into "new and Soviet" as against "old, foreign, and inimical" has a set of villains very much like Gratsiansky. One of them, also a professor — of psychology — resembles Gratsiansky remarkably. He is trying to harm the Soviet authorities; his allegiance is entirely to the old ways of thinking and doing things. To the same category belongs the main villain of Mikhail Sholokhov's novel *Virgin Soil Upturned*. He is an ex-White officer, in hiding in a farmer's house, plotting armed uprisings against the Soviet regime.

When we turn to the villains — and there are many of them — in Venyamin Kaverin's *Searches and Hopes*, we find an entirely different kind of person. Kramov, Skrypachenko, and their allies and followers are not products of an environment alien to Soviet Russia and predating it. They are men nurtured by Soviet life, domesticated in it, belonging entirely to it, and rising within it. Like Gratsiansky, they have chosen science — in their case, medicine and public health — as their field of operation. They have played clever politics in their personal relations and in the institutional structures of Soviet society. They are particularly skilled at profiting from the instrumentalities of terror built into the Soviet system. Their special talent is for "writing," Kaverin says about them several times with bitter irony. By "writing," he explains, he does not mean that they produce works of scientific or artistic literature, but that they incline toward "anonymous works." They pen letters of denunciation against their enemies whom they accuse of various crimes. Even when on occasion their accusations are not believed, a little doubt lingers about the victims; eventually the slanderers secure their removal. They hold meetings in which they debate whom they ought to send to jail, whom to frame; they do not hesitate to bring about executions. Preparing draft after draft of pernicious accusations of sabotage, they go about their business with the care of a conscientious scholar or statesman.

Power is their main motive, together with the advantages accru-

115

ing from it: prestige, material benefits. An important difference between them and Gratsiansky is that they are many. There is nothing of the lonely or isolated evildoer about them. They have an "empire." They put their supporters into positions of power, ruin those who will not play along with them.

They are adept at taking advantage of all the social and political loopholes in Soviet institutional structures which fail to safeguard the rights of the individual and of justice. They could not operate as they do if it were not for the atmosphere of fear surrounding all officials, high and low; a hysterical, witch-hunting obsession with "saboteurs"; the absence of means of legal defense for the accused; an ignoring of rules of evidence; a net of interconnections between the accusers, the judges, and the authorities of appeal; the panic which strikes all citizens on hearing that someone has been arrested, preventing them from testifying on his behalf, and leading them to cut all connections with him, his family, and friends; the uncircumscribed, uncontrolled power of individuals in positions of authority; the impossibility of expressing openly any opposition, not to mention organizing an opposition.

Kaverin's daring in publishing a book containing a detailed picture of the operation of the Kramov-Skrypachenko "empire" is an important step in the breakthrough of the writers in 1956.

Kramov and his allies oppose the efforts of Tatyana Vlasenkova to develop a Soviet version of penicillin, as we saw in an earlier chapter. They denounce and cause the arrest and sentencing of her husband, Andrei. We learn that nine persons had already been arrested in the Institute of Prophylactics, headed by one of the Kramovites, Skrypachenko. The difficulty of helping Andrei after his arrest is increased by the fact that Tatyana does not even know what charges have been made against him or who accused him. The turning point comes when she is visited by Kramov's wife Glafira, who can no longer stand her knowledge of the intrigues in which her husband is engaged. She tells Tatyana who it is that has been persecuting and denouncing Andrei — for his enemies had maintained hypocritically friendly relations with their victims. She also tells her what the accusations had been, bringing with her rough drafts which she has fished out of a wastepaper basket. The charges turn out to be a collection of accusations of sabotage. His enemies blame him for having broken a cholera quarantine with the intention of contaminating the Northern Caucasus and accuse him of having been connected with spies and saboteurs and having introduced a typhus epidemic into the Institute of Prophylactics.

Glafira also reveals that there are two factions among the villains — the new and the old. Kramov belongs to the old group, Skrypachenko to the new. She predicts that the time is coming when the new group will no longer need Kramov and will get rid of him. Kramov is the only genuine scientist among them; they need his reputation to cover them. Soon, however, the ignoramuses brought in by Kramov will be powerful enough to dispense with Kramov. He is too "old-fashioned"; their methods are "simpler." The conspirators are more reckless, ruthless, and powerful than even Tatyana, one of their main victims, had suspected: "You don't know anything yet," Glafira tells her. "Only one thing can help — Kramov's death. Otherwise he will achieve everything regardless — humiliation, annihilation, and death, if not physical, then spiritual. He is an outlaw. He gained all this by robbery — money, a splendid apartment, rugs, furniture, glory, his connections . . . Do you know, there are hundreds of people like them. Even more — thousands. They stick up for each other. They fear and hate each other, and still, how they stick up, how they cover up for each other!"

The new generation of villains promises to be worse even than Kramov. Another character explains, "Kramov with all his bad qualities used to be a man of science and still dimly remembers that. His successors have no past, they have nothing except what he taught them. Those people are capable of crime." Kramov himself does not hesitate to turn everything, even the most recent and important discovery of medical science, to his personal advantage, at the cost of countless people's suffering: "In a word," Tatyana says, "to me the penicillin mold represents painful doubts, vacillation, the bitterness of failures, an idea which I carried around with me for years. And for him — it is a sure-fire trump card, a chance to make people talk about him, to justify advances of which he

117

piled up quite a lot. This means new connections, new glory, new wealth, and he knows very well what to do with money."

In conventional Soviet novels, victims of unjust persecution find ready support among governmental and party officials. Not so in Kaverin's book. The stock scenes of receiving succor from the proper authorities are almost parodied by Kaverin. Tatyana visits a man "with long years of service," who welcomes her with a great show of cordiality. When he learns, however, that she has come to him for help because Andrei had been arrested, his manner becomes a mixture of embarrassment, senility, and confusion. He changes the subject of conversation, rants about the progress of the war, and advises Tatyana to "turn to the government." She asks him: "But how is one to do that?" "Let us think about that," he says, sits down in an armchair, thinks — and falls asleep. That is all the help he renders her.

It is only in June 1953, after the death of Stalin, that Andrei returns a free man. Letters to the Procurator General of Soviet Russia, supported by information supplied by Glafira Kramova, did some good. Kaverin then skips from June 1953 to New Year's Eve, 1956. We find Kramov referred to as "the late Kramov," without any detailed explanation of what happened to him; we do learn that Skrypachenko had been expelled from the Party. The question preoccupying characters on the eve of the year 1956 is whether or not Kramovism is still alive. Some are optimistic; others think Kramovism has not yet been conquered.

One view expressed at the end of the book is that "The new is knocking on all windows and doors, and some people pretend that they do not hear its knocking. You ask me who those people are? The same ones who in postwar years burst not into laboratories, there they had nothing to do, but into various offices, directorates, secretariats. They are the same old Kramovites, although the late boss with his discreetness, with his regard for world science, with his dim recollections that once upon a time he himself was active in the great Russian scientific effort, would probably look among these people like an old-fashioned little fuddy-duddy." The optimist, on the other hand, believes that the Kramovites, "gnashing their teeth, retreat before the spirit of truth and rectitude which cannot fail to conquer. . . . Everything is improving. . . . It is difficult to overestimate the importance of the fact that all those old kinds of struggles about which I do not even want to think — today is a holiday — have vanished irrevocably into the past. . . . Never before did the past have so little significance in comparison with the future." Kaverin, then, presents a picture of villainy far more insidious, widespread, and harmful than Leonov's Gratsiansky. "Kramovism" and "the Kramovites" become for the author himself generic terms for the numerous entrenched "imperialists" in positions of power.

Wisely Kaverin concludes his book with a question — will the Kramovites remain in or return to power, or will a better future come despite the grim past? He leaves no doubt, however, about the horror of the situation as it existed under Stalin, in Kramov's and Skrypachenko's heyday.

Alexander Korneichuk, the Ukrainian playwright, during World War II caused a sensation with his play *The Front* (1942), obviously written with the encouragement of Stalin. The play came out strongly against old-fashioned, World War I-vintage generals who despised such newfangled methods as radio communications, reconnaissance, aerial and tank warfare, and in favor of the younger generation of more recently trained officers.

In 1954 he caused an almost equally great commotion with his play *The Wings*. As usual with Korneichuk, the play in its construction resembles a morality play. Not only do most of the characters have names expressing their nature or occupation (the cowardly, imitative Mr. Sheepish, the gardener Mr. Garden, Mr. Cow and Mr. Cherry, chairmen of collective farms, Mr. Sleepyhead, chairman of the provincial government administration) but the issues are equally schematized. The plot follows a formula. Everything is subordinated to making as clearly and emphatically as possible Korneichuk's main point.

While the complex novelistic art of Kaverin is worlds removed from Korneichuk's naive dramatic manner, Kaverin's choice of a villain — a man high up in Stalinist scientific bureaucracy — is only a short step removed from Korneichuk's. The main purpose of *The Wings* is to expose and pillory the administration of Mr. Sleepyhead, the provincial chairman, and his colleagues. The method used by Korneichuk is to follow the discoveries made about conditions in the province by a new Party secretary, Peter Romodan. Romodan arrives at the place of his new assignment only to find that he is the fourth secretary in five years, nobody expects he will last very long, and people refer to him as the "temporary secretary," while his opposite number, Sleepyhead, is being referred to as "the chief boss." Romodan, however, as every reader or spectator expects, is a man of different mettle than his predecessors. He uncovers Sleepyhead's doings and emerges on top of the heap at the end of the play. What interests Korneichuk is exactly what interests us in our present inquiry: the nature of Sleepyhead's villainy — the details of his nefarious provincial administration.

We learn that he not only is lying down on his job, but makes up for his inefficiency by being dictatorial, shouting at everybody, "making authoritative holes in the sky with his nose," ignoring everything in his province which is going badly, sending in exaggerated accounts of successes, keeping agricultural experts at their city desks, and never going to the country to look at conditions with his own eyes. He is a master at whitewashing bad conditions and beating everybody into line. Romodan finds that the stores are empty, official reports are full of pious quotations from authorities but contain no genuine information, and at meetings speakers are given set speeches to read instead of their own, which would have been full of complaints. Everything is done according to a set pattern.

Behind Sleepyhead's misrule lies a sinister contempt for people, from which springs his reliance on intimidation as his favorite instrument of policy. Sleepyhead despises the people's intelligence. He is quite content to give them lies, window-dressing. When that does not work, he frightens them. He is ready to use any threat in order to strengthen his hold. For example, a person's having been a prisoner of the Germans or a forced laborer in Germany during the war is to him sufficient reason to distrust that person ever after.

By the same token, Sleepyhead does not see why the demands of the people for a better life in the present should be heeded. They can wait — their needs for more food and better consumer goods are not urgent. All strength is put into work for some dim future, for "communism," rather than for the current generation. Behind the play we can sense the pent-up impatience of Soviet citizens whose aspirations for a richer life had been constantly put off by references to future gratifications — always just beyond the horizon. Romodan, Korneichuk's mouthpiece, refutes Sleepyhead's opinions: "The future is born in the present moment. If we do not produce plenty of agricultural products, all our talk about the bright future will be a bunch of prophecies and not a militant program of the party for which philosophers and tractor drivers and all of us must fight daily." The remote Utopian future of communism even becomes a laughingstock. People joke about what it will be like — what will be done with drunkards? Will they receive vodka free of charge? Obviously the present is the only reality to which Korneichuk's characters respond seriously.

In the post-Stalin, post-Beria Russia in which the play is set, people rejoice in the turning of the wheel of fortune, which has brought about the jailing of the former oppressors themselves. "The man who threatened Anna with a concentration camp was flown off to Moscow the day after Beria was arrested, and now he is sitting in jail." Grief is felt over the Stalinist days: "How much evil, suffering, tears, were inflicted on people by the distrust which was spread by that gang in the guise of 'alertness'! They pulled the wool over our eyes and we believed them. And how we believed. . . . Never again will that nightmare return."

People are no longer to be begged or pressured into accomplishments. "We'll find the key to it [persuading people to work] in man's soul. When engineers understand what a great honor it is to work in the Machine Tractor Stations, in these historical times of our country, what hopes the Central Committee of the Party is placing in them, they will come forward eagerly. . . . Caress a man and he will move mountains." The hero of the play replaces Sleepyhead's terror with trust and kindness. Thus, too, is the title of the play

121

explained. The new view of life supplies the people with so much truth and strength "that we have grown wings." "It seems to me," Romodan says, "that I am flying over the whole earth."

The Wings may be an oversimplified allegory, resembling a fairy tale. But the suggestion it carries and the fact that it was published in 1954 and produced in many Russian theaters are significant. The dictatorship of Sleepyhead is a microcosm reflecting the contempt for man and the criminal conduct in the macrocosm of the Kremlin. The villain of the piece is the governmental official, presented not as exceptional, but as typical and well established, capable of outlasting many successive Party secretaries. The admission of guilt, too, is collective, not exceptional and individual. Romodan says, "Didn't we all see the hideous things which were going on? Didn't we think about them? But we shut our eyes to them; we were doing more following than leading, as we ought to do."

Korneichuk is attacking inhuman governmental oppression and shouting his hope for a democratic, humanistic, free ordering of the people's affairs.

A petty dictator in the ranks of ministerial bureaucracy, Poludin in Alexander Shtein's play *A Personal Case* (1954), complements Korneichuk's Sleepyhead. Poludin occupies the key position of head of the personnel section of a ministry. He persecutes Khlebnikov, a hard-working, excellent engineer. By means of unsubstantiated charges of disloyalty, Poludin succeeds in having Khlebnikov dismissed from his job and expelled from the Communist Party. It is only through the efforts of a naval officer who is an old friend of Khlebnikov's and of a woman party official that Khlebnikov is vindicated and Poludin exposed.

As in Korneichuk's play, the villain is the main source of interest of the drama. As a Soviet critic wrote, Poludin demonstrates "the terrible power of 'papers,' of those people who knew how to turn a questionnaire into an instrument of terror." His manner of operating is shown in a scene in which he instructs a Party official how to phrase the accusation against Khlebnikov. He twists insignificant, innocent facts into ominous offenses. Khlebnikov brought some German medals home from the war as souvenirs. This is written

122

down as "smuggling Fascist propaganda across the border." Khlebnikov recommended the employment of an engineer who has since been arrested; he also spent some time in Germany, with the Russian occupation authorities, in the same years during which the arrested engineer was in Germany. This is taken as further evidence of sinister collusion between the two men, even though there is no indication they ever even saw each other in Germany. The charge against Khlebnikov, as dictated by Poludin, reads: "Gross infraction of governmental security, the lack of watchfulness, participation in the hiring and in aiding and abetting Dymnikov, now under arrest . . . falsity and lack of honesty toward the Party." Any objections to his wording and his farfetched deductions are brushed aside by Poludin as evidence of "lack of unity in the office," or as incompatible with the need for "clarity" and "sharpness."

Poludin also conducts meetings undemocratically. He speaks for forty minutes and allows only ten minutes to others; some people are not permitted to express their opinion at all. Anybody who defends Khlebnikov is accused of "liberalism" and "abetting the enemy." Poludin calls one opponent "a liberal with rotten innards," and threatens the Party members with "finding themselves in a shameful position if they do not expel Khlebnikov in time." Later Poludin's activity is summed up fairly when he is said to have "created an unhealthy and un-communistic atmosphere of persecution in which it is impossible to ascertain the truth."

We learn that personal motives lie behind Poludin's persecution of Khlebnikov. He is jealous of Khlebnikov's competence as an engineer; once, furthermore, he had asked Khlebnikov to include him in a special group of engineers working as consultants and Khlebnikov turned him down.

Two other facts emerge from Poludin's tyranny of denunciation. The first is the importance of whether or not a man's friends stand up for him when he is under attack. Most of Khlebnikov's friends do not. Later, when he is vindicated, they are ashamed for their cowardice and apologize. "A bucket is particularly valuable during a fire," he tells them. From Shtein's presentation, it is clear that many Soviet citizens recognize the question of how to behave when someone is accused of subversive activity as a frequent dilemma.

The second revelation concerns the importance of Party membership. Shtein is almost mawkish in stressing what a tragedy the expulsion from the Party is to Khlebnikov. In a melodramatic scene he presents Khlebnikov's grief when he is asked to turn in his Party membership card. Here Shtein may be partly falling in with official adulation of the Party, but there seems to be more to it than mere lip-service. The Party, not as it really exists, manipulated by officials like Poludin, but a mythical, abstract "Party" standing for all that is good, for unselfish service to society, for self-sacrificing work for the sake of the country and the future generations — an idealistic construct — seems to be valued all the more for the unjust persecutions by the various Poludins. People like Khlebnikov have to have some center to their lives — something in which to trust. As Ignaty, Tina's husband in Galina Nikolaeva's *Battle on the Way*, urges her to do, Khlebnikov puts his faith in the "Party" in this ideal sense. All personal honor is tied up with the Party. "What would be my life without the Party?" Khlebnikov says.

No wonder he is in difficulties when he finds himself expelled from the Party which had meant everything to him. He tries to make a fine distinction between the actual Party which rejected him and a theoretical Party. He refuses to feel "hurt" or "injured" by the Party. The people at the top — the Central Committee — will help him. "Today, at the meeting, the people were deceived. But it is impossible to deceive the Party."

Shtein maneuvers the plot of his play so as to justify Khlebnikov's trust. Poludin is castigated, Khlebnikov rewarded at the end by being restored to membership and even promoted in his job. But meanwhile the play has revealed the profound damage which can be done by an official who uses threats, takes advantage of the proneness to look for traitors and spies, easily imputes evil motives to his enemies, and stoops to serious political charges against those who will not do him favors.

A villain similar to Sleepyhead and Poludin is found in the first play of a young dramatist, Alexander Volodin. Bibichev, the head

124

of the Young Communist League (Komsomol) organization in a factory, completes our triptych of Party and governmental officials presented as negative characters. *Factory Girl* (1956) has been — and still is — the subject of lively discussions, pro and con. The main Russian journal concerned with drama, *Theater* (*Teatr*), devoted space in several consecutive monthly issues to a debate about the play.

Zhenka, the heroine, is a simple, rather flighty, fun-loving, free-spoken young girl, whom Bibichev chooses as his victim. The casual callousness with which accusations are fabricated is illustrated by the circumstance which is the beginning of Zhenka's troubles. The Komsomol organization received from a newspaper, the *Komsomol Pravda*, a request for an article entitled "She Fills Us with Shame." It was to be "about a girl who runs around to dances, who takes her Komsomol membership lightly . . . In sum, about the moral situation." Zhenka does not care what she says; she shocks people by her frankness. Since somebody has to be, it is she who is chosen as the subject of the desired article for the newspaper. The remainder of the play is a duel between her — appearing in the role of the "fighter for truth" — and Bibichev, who stands for hypocrisy and bureaucracy.

The presentation of the unpolitical, plain-spoken Zhenka as heroine and of the prig Bibichev as villain aroused much displeasure among the Stalinist critics. The play found its defenders, however. One of them accused the critics of sounding like Bibichev. Their attacks on the playwright, he wrote, could be entitled "He Fills Us with Shame"; they betrayed the same bureaucratic and strait-laced intolerance as was satirized in Bibichev. The play, this critic wrote, applied to a target even broader than the Komsomol. "The point here is not in the quality of the leadership of the Komsomol in general, but rather that the Party, and the Komsomol, and the labor unions, are at present shaking off bureaucracy." Thus a Soviet critic was able, in 1957, to make the connection between the deterrent example of one Komsomol official in a play — and the thousands of Soviet leaders in various important spheres of life, in the Party and in the labor unions.

It is not accidental that the villainous Party or governmental official has been illustrated by examples from three plays, rather than novels. During the period with which we are concerned the Soviet dramatist had his hand strengthened by the nature of his medium. If he could get his play produced, he could then draw on the support of his audiences. In their turn, critics favoring the play could refer to its success on the stage, thus providing a counterpoise to the official or Stalinist unfavorable criticism. B. Lvov, the producer of *The Factory Girl* in Moscow, for example, took as his target a critic who had pompously written about the playwright, "Our young men and women perhaps will forgive you all your offenses against truth . . ." and answered: "The idea doesn't enter our young men's and women's heads whether to 'forgive' or 'not to forgive' Volodin. They simply fill the theaters to the last row, roar with laughter, give stormy applause to almost every line, and feverishly discuss the show during intermission." This is an advantage which novelists do not have. Their public cannot make its views felt collectively and palpably. The theatrical public fails to attend boring plays which misrepresent reality; it fills to overflowing and applauds plays which have something important to say about Soviet life. Judged by these criteria, the three villains Sleepyhead, Poludin, and Bibichev embody characteristics of Soviet officialdom which must have been notorious among millions of people.

In the three best, most provocative, and most discussed novels published in Russia between 1954 and 1957, Ehrenburg's *The Thaw*, Dudintsev's *Not by Bread Alone*, and Nikolaeva's *A Battle on the Way*, the characters cast as villains are the typical successes of Soviet Russian life — self-made captains of industry, top-flight, honored, dashing directors of factories. These characters belong to the new intelligentsia which Stalin undertook to create for the purposes of the country's rapid industrialization. They are very different from the occasional *spets*, the hated and distrusted "specialist" of foreign origin or trained in prerevolutionary days, who was denigrated in Soviet books of the twenties and thirties.

Ehrenburg's Zhuravlev, Dudintsev's Drozdov, and Nikolaeva's

Valgan are three men produced by the new educational, social, and industrial system of the Five-Year Plan. On the surface they are Soviet Horatio Algers. They work hard; they have succeeded and are on their way up; their plants appear to operate splendidly. They, their assistants, and their factories are awarded special premiums and bonuses, as well as banners, orders, and titles. Yet the three novelists do not hold out these factory managers to their readers' admiration, but rather unmask them and declare them dangerous and evil. What are the true characteristics of these three men which account for the authors' attitudes toward them? What explains the astonishing reversal of earlier official Soviet values?

First we notice that the Soviet authors give even these devils their due. Drozdov has one important positive characteristic in common with Valgan and Zhuravlev – and this is an important point of distinction between him and such villains as Gratsiansky and Kramov; he works hard and efficiently. These factory directors have risen to the top at least partly on their merits. They are good engineers; they love their jobs; they excel at driving the men under them to work as hard as they do. These are truly the "builders," in Dudintsev's image, the "ants" working industriously at the expansion of Russian economic might. It is made clear that their finest hour came during the war, when, with extra-stringent means, they squeezed the last drop of effort out of their men and out of themselves.

Their next important trait is partly a function of their skill as production men: they are hard. They have no pity for others or for themselves. Their hearts are as calloused as their hands. From their single-minded eagerness to succeed as industrial tycoons follows a string of vices and abuses, culminating in serious crimes. The energy of these men makes bullies out of them. They shout at their inferiors; they do not hesitate to strike them. Valgan in particular can be dictatorial. All three are inhuman, robot-like, monstrous.

Next, they are not content with legitimate successes in fulfilling production quotas, but, adept at taking advantage of the Soviet system of incentive rewards, they cheat wherever possible. They put their own record first, and everything else second. They want to

127

mark up the highest figures for their factory where they count the most: in production results. Thus Zhuravlev pours all capital into expansion of productive capacity, ignoring the need for housing for his workers. An apartment construction project has been authorized, the funds for it appropriated, but Zhuravlev postpones it year after year, since he prefers to watch the curve of industrial production go up, rather than see his men move out of their filthy, unsafe quarters. This is the eventual cause of his downfall. A storm tears down the workers' hovels and Zhuravlev's neglect is publicly exposed. He is removed as manager of the factory.

Valgan in *A Battle on the Way* is so eager for honors and rewards that he permits a defective tractor model to be submitted for a Stalin Prize, although several tractors of that line had suffered the same serious and dangerous accident, proving a defect in their construction. On the other hand, while he strives to shine on the honor list of successful factory directors, Valgan does not want anybody under him to break a record of production, or receive favorable publicity. When a young man, without authorization from Valgan, does develop a new technique which makes possible much speedier work than previously, Valgan, far from rejoicing over the improvement and the resulting gains to Soviet economy, illegally punishes the young man by assigning him to work where the pay is small and the quota assigned very high so that premiums for surpassing the quota are impossible to gain. The young man protests that according to regulations, anyone who invents a speedier way of working is to be rewarded by being kept for six months on the same production quota as he had before his innovation, so that he can reap the benefit of the extra income for easily overfulfilling his old quota. Valgan admits that such a regulation exists, but adds that there is no rule prohibiting the man from being transferred to another job. There seems to be no appeal from such an evasion of the spirit of the regulations.

The factory managers offend against economic regulations in many other ways. They pad their production figures, not being content to let the record speak for itself, cutting corners left and right to gain extra premiums and "good marks" on their record. Valgan, for example, used artificially lowered norms of production. Toward the end the month he listed as "assembled" tractors which were not yet completed, and through this subterfuge overfulfilled the plan. In reporting the quantity of defective goods produced, he subtracted the "legal" percentage, the quantity of rejects and irregulars allowed for in the production plan. Drozdov suppressed for years a superior invention of a pipe-casting machine.

Still more villainous than their breaches of economic and industrial rules are their brutal ways of dealing with people. Being eager for power, these men use any means to get their will. Naturally they take advantage of the special opportunities available in the conditions of Soviet life. They are ready to impute evil political motives to their adversaries. They readily accuse their enemies of "economic sabotage." When Zhuravlev in *The Thaw* wishes to combat Sokolovsky, he takes advantage of the fact that Sokolovsky's wife years before left him, married a foreigner, and is now living with Sokolovsky's daughter in Belgium. Zhuravlev insinuates that of course one cannot fully trust a person with "connections" and relatives abroad.

At conferences, these managers are skilled in packing committees, in depriving their opponents of an opportunity to speak, and in presenting their own case as favorably as possible, if need be fraudulently. In these techniques they resemble their political colleagues, the Sleepyheads, Poludins, and Bibichevs.

The novelists felt free to generalize about the characteristics of these villains and to explain where they come from, what caused them, and what could be done to remove them and to prevent their return. Nikolaeva supplies two explanations of what makes the evil men such as they are. The first cause she gives is their combination of "worship of authority" and "fear." They ascribe to others their own thirst for power; paranoiacally, they see rivals and enemies in everybody. They fear signs both of friendship, which might be demanding, and of enmity, which might be aggressive and cunning. They detest cordiality, openness, human closeness. Thus they are afraid of others — and react by trying to manipulate them through terror. The second explanation is that these men "adapt their thinking to the point of automatism." They have no beliefs of their own. Whatever is momentarily dominant becomes their own opinion. One of them was in favor of one hundred per cent collectivization, at any cost, thinking that to be the ruling view. As soon as Stalin's speech "Dizzy with Success" appeared, he attacked bitterly what he had believed the day before. Others changed their views honestly, after an inner struggle, but this character "knew no such imperfection in his adapting mechanism. . . . He wanted to become like everybody and to forget that yesterday he prided himself on his different view." They are dangerous because of their opportunism.

Nikolaeva shows that there is a correspondence between the manner of behavior of these men on their own level in industry and the manner in which things are done on the highest level, in politics. The heyday of Stalinism was their heyday. The thaw after Stalin's death is the beginning of their decline. Their dependence on authoritarian aloofness is illustrated when the Kremlin is opened to visits by the people: they panic. One of them "went to the Kremlin on business. He was accustomed to see the Kremlin inaccessible, solemn, deserted. To enter it was an honor and a privilege. And now, in this same Kremlin, there are crowds of unknown men and women, boys and girls, they crawl in every corner, take snapshots with their cameras. 'The much-populated, accessible Kremlin,' that's what it used to be called once upon a time, he remembered. But when? During the Civil War, a time of disorder. . . . To return to the past? No. . . . He looked for the customary marble grandeur and saw nothing sculpturesque, monumental. He saw people here. They could argue. The Bakhirevs and Kurganovs [his democratic enemies] were permitted to enter these halls. He felt like warning: 'People will abuse this ease of access.'"

These men, Drozdov, Valgan, Zhuravlev, were produced by conditions of Oriental despotism on the top of the pyramid of power. The relaxation after the death of Stalin frightens them. They are afraid of the people. Through their behavior they demonstrate that they had become a self-enclosed ruling class; they react to the "interval of freedom" as if it were a second revolution, a new civil war. They are afraid of democracy. Plurality of opinions and arguments strike them as anarchy — and as indications of their loss of the monopoly of power.

Ovechkin, a Soviet author who specializes in stories with a farm setting, has summed up the common bad qualities of the contemporary Russian man under two headings. Our three villains combine all of them. The negative characteristics are, first, those arising from the desire to do everything more quickly than others and without waiting for anybody else, and, second, those designated by three Russian slang terms, *shkurnik, perestrakhovshchik,* and a Party-member *obyvatel.*

The first characteristic we have seen in operation: the several villains show eagerness to break production norms, by means fair or foul, and a drive to assert themselves by stepping on all others.

The second group of traits requires an explanation. *Shkurnik* is derived from the word for "skin." A "skinner" is a man who cares for nothing except saving his own skin — an opportunist, someone playing it safely and selfishly. *Perestrakhovshchik* means an "over-insurer." It is somebody who wants to "insure" that he will negotiate successfully the system of production quotas, norms, premiums, bonuses, raw material allocations. He "insures" himself by hoarding, concealing supplies he already has, and underestimating possible production so as to be assigned the smallest quota possible, which he then can easily achieve or surpass. *Obyvatel* is a Russian term for a bourgeois, in the pejorative sense: someone small, petty, usually puritanical, philistine, narrow-minded, cowardly. The traits of an *obyvatel* are clearest in Bibichev in *The Factory Girl.* Zhuravlev, Valgan, and Drozdov show many of the characteristics of a *shkurnik* and a *perestrakhovshchik.*

The final situation in which the author leaves his villains at the end of the book is important. Our three novelists are far from optimistic. They show the villains as having suffered reverses which are only temporary. Zhuravlev has been removed from the factory where he did so much harm to the workers, but in Part II of the book he is already beginning to rise to the top at a factory in a remote part of the country, probably practicing the same old tricks, with the same success.

Ehrenburg does not have anything specific to say about how to prevent men like Zhuravlev from acquiring power or from becoming corrupt. The vague suggestion is made that more watchfulness is necessary, that education must be enlisted in order to produce men with higher standards of ethics. But Ehrenburg suggests no institutional structure, no reform, no change in society which would provide checks and balances as guarantees against the excessive power of these "little Stalins." He seems to trust hopefully to improvements due solely to the death of Stalin and the removal of Beria — and to the rather amorphous powers of education and enlightened public opinion. He does not deem it necessary (or perhaps printable in Soviet Russia?) to explain through what channels and with what legal or institutional safeguards education and public opinion could find salutary application.

On the other hand, Ehrenburg says some daring things about the origin of evil men. His Sokolovsky explains to a friend what he thinks were the causes responsible for making Zhuravlev what he is: "The trouble of course was not in Zhuravlev. You insist on branding a man as if he were a thief or a toady from the cradle up. A lot depends on upbringing, on environment."

The same question of who is to blame for moral corruption is dramatized by Ehrenburg in connection with another negative character, the painter Volodya Pukhov, who displays characteristics similar to Zhuravlev's but in another sphere of activity, art. Volodya paints tawdry but popular pictures of smiling Pioneers in summer camps, groups of happy workers, prosperous executives. His successes contrast with the misfortunes of a superior, true artist, Saburov, whose paintings no one buys, who lives in misery with his crippled wife, and who allows only artistic conscience to guide him in painting. Volodya lives not in opposition to but in accordance with the official demands of Soviet art, by whose standards he is a success: he is prolific, follows the taste of socialist realism, sells many pictures on socially approved subjects, and receives much praise. His failure is inward, human and artistic. Ehrenburg broaches the question of Volodya's dishonesty: why is he a bad, corrupt, opportunistic artist? Volodya himself muses about this at one point: "I missed the boat in everything — in love, work, life. What have I dreamed about? Perhaps only about the prize. . . . It is not my fault. It is the times we are living in. It isn't important how we paint, the main thing is to hit on a subject not a year too soon and not a year too late. If a campaign against alcoholism is on, perhaps a drunken daddy who can't get the key into the keyhole and a Pioneer daughter who watches with disapproval."

Later he decides not to blame the age he lives in: "Difficult times? Of course. But have there ever been easy times? There exist only persons who behave badly, like me . . . the trouble is not in the times." Still the effects of Soviet environment on the painter as well as on the factory manager are shown to be pernicious.

Dudintsev at the end of *Not by Bread Alone* shows the villains, Drozdov and others, defeated on the single issue of Lopatkin's new pipe-casting machine, but otherwise still solidly entrenched in power. They are still publicly honored; they have suffered only one exceptional and temporary reverse. The forces responsible for them, Dudintsev makes clear, are not alien to Soviet society, but inherent in its very nature. The Drozdovs are produced by the conditions of Soviet industrial society: its bureaucratic organizations, the lack of checks and limitations on dictatorial individuals, absence of proper safeguards. The great rush to industrialize had as its by-product "empire-building" by unscrupulous lovers of power. Drozdov's career was made possible and even probable by the Soviet system.

What does Dudintsev propose as countermeasures? He is somewhat less vague than Ehrenburg on this point. He, too, sees the need for a vast re-education of the Soviet public, but he does not leave it at that. At the end of the book his hero, Lopatkin, decides that he may have to go into politics in order to continue his struggle. Fighting as one scientist among many, one engineer amidst the complexity of technological industrial organizations, seems to him to have limited possibilities. A more basic reform is necessary — one which can only be brought about from a position at the heart, not at the fringes, of power: by working through the Communist Party.

Galina Nikolaeva links her villains to Stalinism more clearly than the other two novelists. She makes the connection frequently and explicitly. Some of the factors productive of big and small Stalins and Berias had already been swept away, she believes, with the changes in the Kremlin; but the people must be re-educated in order to hate and struggle against authoritarianism on the grass-roots level. People like Valgan are not wholly evil in themselves; they are complex, she says, mixed good and evil. Which half of them will gain dominance, whether the good or the bad, depends on the environment surrounding them and on the checks placed on them. They are potentially capable of being either villains or heroes. In Stalinist Russia, she declares quite openly, their environment was such that their evil side grew strong, their good side atrophied. Galina Nikolaeva proposes to place the Valgans of Russia under perpetual and close supervision. She writes about her chief villain: "He is a complicated, contradictory man. . . . When a man like Valgan lives closely together with the community under its many-eyed and perpetual control, the vampire in him withers away, rolls itself up, crawls deep down, loses its strength. But this man found himself not among human beings, but outside of their health-giving life, outside their many-eyed control. And the vampire acquired strength, stretched out its tentacles, changing his face and smile, his movements and his habits, his manner of life and even his manner of thinking."

Galina Nikolaeva is quite practical in her suggestions on how to make sure the Valgans would not again be corrupted and enabled (or encouraged) to acquire power in the future. She implements her general comments by quite detailed specific proposals. She is not content merely to ask for an idealistic re-education of everybody in Russia. She wants to surround man with incentives which will lead him in the right direction. Her plan includes both the stick and the carrot. Far more realistic than the other novelists, she recommends, through the characters who are the heroes of her book, that man's self-interest be enlisted as well as his idealism. She even wants to use the profit-motive. The economy must be reorganized so that it will not pay to cheat on quotas, to underestimate productive possibilities, to hoard supplies needed by another factory. Industrial planning must include financial rewards for the efficient administrator.

In moving from the earlier group of negative characters to the last, we followed the writers' shift in emphasis from individuals inherently evil (exceptional, isolated bad men, or persons harmful because alien or opposed to the Soviet system) to men very typical of the Soviet system, not evil in spite of the Soviet way of life but rather because of it — direct products of it, in important respects actually corrupted by it. The blame, daringly and provocatively, was placed at the door of basic Soviet institutions.

The next logical step is to emphasize the individual villain still less and the causal factor of the Soviet environment still more. This is exactly what we find in a group of stories published in 1956 and 1957, of which Daniel Granin's "Personal Convictions," Nikolai Gorbunov's "The Mistake," Nikolai Zhdanov's "A Trip Home," and Alexander Yashin's "The Levers" are typical. In all of them, no one character can be considered "evil" or "villainous" in the sense in which the terms apply to our earlier examples. The negative characters are more victims than offenders, more sinned against than sinning. The blame is shifted altogether to the system, to Soviet conditions of life. The stories are still saturated with "negativeness," with a sense of something very wrong. But the evil inheres in the Soviet environment, not in special characteristics of a few individuals.

In Granin's "Personal Convictions", as we saw in Chapter II, the head of the research laboratory, Minaev, will not permit Olkhovsky to publish an embarrassing but true article, because it would cause "complications" through its criticism of an important academician. He fails to lift a finger to help Olkhovsky, who later finds himself unjustly persecuted because of his views. Drozdov may seem to resemble Minaev inasmuch as he obstructs Lopatkin's invention of a pipe-casting machine and runs interference for the important academician Avdiev. Yet Minaev is a character very different from Drozdov. In many ways he is not a villain at all. His heart is in the right place; he would like to help Olkhovsky. Furthermore, he thinks of himself as a champion of lost causes, as a fighter for the underdog and a critic of powerful but unjust bureaucrats. We realize that Minaev is a frustrated hero, a passive character, a victim, rather than an active doer of evil deeds.

Like Olkhovsky, Minaev thinks a great deal about principles. "You like to throw around that word principles," he tells the young engineer. "But try to put it into action. Earn the right and means to put it into action. Yes, Comrade Olkhovsky, put it into effect, not into words. To do that, one has to sacrifice a few things." At first the reader may be inclined to consider Minaev the cause of Olkhovsky's troubles. But as he reads along in the story, he realizes that the director is a pathetic, not a negative, character. The words just quoted describe the tragedy of his life. He has sacrificed too many things — everything important, in fact — in his effort to rise high enough to "put his principles into effect." In the process of climbing the Soviet social and bureaucratic ladder, with the help of what he considered purely temporary and tactical discretion and pretense of collaboration with the men in power, he actually lost his soul. No position will ever be sufficiently high for him to dare speak his mind; at every stage there will be mighty reasons for playing ball with the powers that be, for postponing his rebellion still further. He will never say or do anything for his principles.

"Personal Convictions" is a sad, effectively presented story of a Soviet official's discovery of the fact that he was not and never would be a man of courage and that he had irrevocably sold his conscience in return for worldly success. What makes it relevant in a discussion of villains in Soviet fiction despite the absence of a clearly defined personal villain in the story is that the author is insistently calling the reader's attention to a great waste which has taken place and that he is by implication pointing an accusing finger at the cause of the pathetic deterioration of a human being and the countless others who are like him. The cause is not any one person or group of persons. Granin is blaming the Soviet social structure of authority which rewards and promotes men who sell out, crushes and ostracizes men who remain true to their convictions. The villain of Granin's story is a power-structure which induces all but the most reckless and courageous men to compromise their principles, to invent excuses for themselves — and carry on an endless game of kowtowing to authority. The story is steeped in a sense of the resulting moral corruption and human loss.

Nikolai Gorbunov's "The Mistake," subtitled "A Monologue of a Professor," is in many ways similar to "Personal Convictions." It, too, deals with a moment of self-realization on the part of a middle-aged man, and its central theme is also the corruption of idealistic, well-meaning men, who are outwardly successes in terms of Soviet values but inwardly have paid the price of moral degeneracy.

Gorbunov presents an eminent professor of geography at the University of Moscow, an academician, who is spending a sleepless night reflecting on the entire course of his life. The son of a semi-illiterate country blacksmith, he was sent, through a series of coincidences, to a university and, thanks to the Soviet system, has now reached the pinnacle of success. He is a respected, well-paid scholar. Yet his nocturnal meditation is caused by the fact that although his life seems to be the incarnation of a Soviet rags-to-riches story, or, as he puts it, "a song," still there seems to be something seriously wrong: he feels a stranger to himself and doubts the purpose of his whole life. As we follow the course of his reminiscences, we come to understand what this "mistake" had been. Like Minaev, the professor was forced to compromise and to give up his convictions. It started with his dissertation, in which he attacked the views of an established professor. When he refused to remove the embarrassing, undiplomatic passages, he was given "the treatment." For one year he held out, while a whispering campaign raged against him. After that, he gave in, changed the dissertation as he was asked, received his degree, and again was considered an intelligent "comrade on the way up," a man of great promise. His career ever since, he now comes to see, has been compounded of time-serving weakness. This was brought home to him recently in a bus, where he overheard a couple of his students talking about him without noticing his presence. One of them told the other, who was writing his dissertation with the professor, that "he is a typical conservative" and advised him to work with another professor "who is more of a man of principle."

The professor, like Minaev, now thinks to himself: "All my life I have thought of myself as a fighter for what is new — and I have ended up among the conservatives. . . . In place of fresh winds, far horizons, and eager public work I have worked . . . within a narrow circle, amidst a chase after authority, self-protection, friendly favors and concessions, the fighting around science, a war with a bitter admixture of ambition and money interests." He thinks of various incidents of his life which now strike him as disillusioning. He sees his field of specialization as a huge lake divided into little sections allotted to various professors as their personal "duchies" which they guard jealously. Any attempt to "break into their magic circle" is countered by "a storm of telephone calls, rejections of dissertations, annihilating reviews in newspapers." He, too, plays the game. He has his own little corner of the Far Eastern and Eastern Sea which is recognized as his own, inviolable specialty. The wheel has swung full circle, since the days of his own iconoclastic dissertation, for now when a young student's dissertation attacks one of his articles, he calls up his friends — and the dissertation is modified.

Gorbunov's story is an artful, melancholy study of a man who is coming to doubt the worth of his whole life. It is an inconclusive story. In the morning the professor moves on with the daily routine of his life. No solution is offered, nothing has happened — except in the professor's mind.

The professor, again, while he appears a victimizer to the young, is also a victim. The fault lies in the chimera-like system of Soviet scholarship. The consequences most bewailed by Gorbunov are the wounds dealt to men who once were eager, bright, filled with principles and a desire to struggle for justice and truth.

The two other stories in this group indict not the world of technology or scholarship, but an equally large, generalized, multiple target — and a still more idolized one in Soviet Russia: the sacrosanct Communist Party itself and the governmental officialdom. True, they do not attack the Party or government as a whole. Their attack is selective and limited in purpose. It aims at the practices, and the consequences of those practices, of Party officials on the lower levels — of the district or city organization. Still, Zhdanov's and Yashin's daring is sufficient to arouse our admiration.

In Nikolai Zhdanov's "A Trip Home," a successful city bureaucrat, Varygin, receives word of the death in the country of his aged mother, whom he has failed to visit for six years. He takes a train to the village where she lived and is to be buried. His visit begins as a retracing of his own childhood days and turns into a journey of discovery of the conditions of life of the rural population: "The idea painfully struck him that his mother had suffered from want."

Life on the farm is much more old-fashioned and wretched than it had seemed from Varygin's office, where he was looked after by an efficient secretary, attended meetings, and studied official reports. The villagers look at him from across a wide gulf: "They say you are one of the leaders." Some assure him that his mother had been well off — she even received sugar a few times a year. Others take the opportunity to overwhelm him with their complaints. They must make excessive compulsory deliveries of produce; they have to send off so much grain that none is left for themselves after springtime.

The conflict between the people and the political-bureaucratic ruling class is clearest in Varygin's conversation with a local engineer, who tells him, "In our region more than half of the nineteen collective farms are doing poorly. The harvest is small, people work unwillingly, they eat badly." Official optimism is attacked: "The village would be much better off if there were fewer government cheerer-uppers. It is necessary to overcome difficulties, not hush them up." The city man "felt neither willingness nor strength to examine all that the engineer told him and that he had seen in the course of the day."

The complacency of a ruler collides with the discouraging harshness of the actual life of the underlings. The story reveals the contradiction between the uninformed optimism of the bureaucratic elite and the wretched life of farm laborers squeezed by demands from above. Zhdanov's story ends with the official's return to town, pleased to escape the unpleasant realities he had witnessed. "With satisfaction he imagined in his mind's eye that tomorrow he would walk into his warm, well-furnished study and sit down in an armchair behind his desk."

Zhdanov is not representing Varygin as a bad man but as a weak man, far removed from the facts of Soviet life and partly responsible for them. Sheltered by the bulwark erected around themselves by the rulers of the country, he is glad to issue commands which make life miserable for the common people and to appease all qualms by resorting to official, optimistic clichés. The story portrays the governmental bureaucracy from the country people's point of view as an alien, possibly hostile, certainly indifferent and privileged group.

Alexander Yashin's "The Levers" is an equally bold exposure of conditions in the country. A group of Party members on a collective farm complain bitterly about the officials at the Party district office, their handling of the Communists on the grass-roots level, and their failure to understand the farmers' difficulties. The farmers dislike being treated like "levers," mere tools of the Party officials one step higher. The secretary of the district organization had told them, "Carry out the Party line. You are now our levers in the village." The collective farm men complain about him: "He doesn't listen to people. He decided everything by himself. He thinks the Party would lose authority if he talked to people simply, like a human being. . . . Our leaders in the District have forgotten how to talk to the people. . . . As long as there is no confidence in the simple peasant on the collective farm, there will be no real order. We'll see a lot of trouble yet. They write about us 'a new human being has made his appearance.' True, he has. 'The collective farm has transformed the peasant.' True, it has transformed him. The peasant is no longer the same. Good. So now they ought to trust this peasant. He too has some sense. They must not only teach us, but also listen to us. Go and disagree with them at the District office. They will give you advice, a recommendation; but it will be no advice, it will be an order."

The story shows that the simple people feel a clear line separates them from the next higher echelon of Party workers. They wish to be trusted, consulted, listened to; they resent being ordered about and considered mere tools. They yearn for warm, personal treatment. The real irony of the story emerges toward its end. For after complaining about the undemocratic, stereotyped treatment meted out by the district officials, the same group of men constitute themselves into a Party meeting — and immediately change for the worse. They actually become mere "levers." They repeat what they had been told to say by the district headquarters, losing the genuine humanity and pride they had shown in their earlier informal session.

Then the Party meeting is over; and as soon as that happens, they drop the Party roles and begin complaining again. Yashin leaves no doubt about where his sympathies lie. His concluding sentence describes the farmers who reassumed their plain non-Party selves: "Again they were pure, cordial, direct people, people, not levers."

Yashin reverses the Stalinist dogma according to which the Party uplifts people and guides them wisely in their personal and group affairs. Yashin's Party abuses people, treats them impersonally, bosses them, and, like the authorities in Zhdanov's story, has little information about or interest in their problems. By assuming the role of Party members, the men, instead of being uplifted, descend to a lower level. The Party and Party membership are represented by Yashin in the negative role of dehumanizing agents.

When we review the qualities most of the literary villains have in common, ignoring for the time being the differences between them, we arrive at a rather long list of unpleasant traits. In one way or another, most of the negative characters are selfish. Consciously or unconsciously, they have the characteristics of *meshchanstvo* or of the *obyvatel*: they are stuffy, narrow-minded, priggish, conceited, bourgeois in the bad sense of the word. They are materialistic in caring for television sets, summer cottages, cars, money. They do not bother their heads over the sufferings of the common people; they are quite willing to extend the people's sacrifices indefinitely, since they can salve their consciences by saying that all is being done for the good of communism; it is inevitable anyway; and they — the elite — are meanwhile not at all badly off.

Some of the villains frame innocent victims, and send their rivals to prison camps or to the firing squad. Their lack of humanity is particularly striking. They are robots, with no time for such luxuries as love, art, an emotional life.

Quite distinctly, they are the upper class. They represent a new elite, a new group of rulers. To some of the Soviet authors we have been considering, the worst thing about the villains is that they pervert something noble — the Party and its ideals. This seems much more serious to the novelists than the damage which the villains incidentally cause to Russian industry and economy. The worst among the negative characters are those who are prominent and admirable by the criteria of Soviet life. The fact that people like them are villains puts into doubt the whole structure of outward appearances by which the Russian people have been encouraged to judge a man's success or failure.

Stories like "Personal Convictions" and "The Mistake" give the impression of approaching tragedies because on the one hand they concentrate on a moment of perception by the character into what had happened to him in the past (sometimes over a long period of time), and on the other hand there is irony in the reversal of good intentions. The professor in "The Mistake," Minaev in "Personal Convictions," and Varygin in "A Trip Home" all meant well; they were firmly convinced that their lives were noble as well as fortunate and successful. Yet they find in the course of the action that their lives have actually been devoted to something ignoble and, worst of all, that there is no way out. They must continue in the same way as before, now accompanied by the knowledge of the shameful waste and defeat of the noblest aspirations of their lives, and at least in the case of the professor and Minaev, with bitter disillusionment about the conditions of existence established in the name of the Party in whose aims they had devoutly believed.

The most tragic characters in these stories of evil are the idealists. They hold images of themselves as heroes, as workers for the people. They are habituated to think of themselves as builders of a fine new society, but a shadow has fallen across their lives. Some self-deception started them on the wrong track. In order to maintain or improve their position, they had to compromise; their careers have gone astray irreversibly.

Another feature which they share is the contrast between the appearance and the reality of their lives. The appearance is that their lives are, as the professor put it in Zhdanov's story, "songs" of Soviet success. The reality is that they have lowered themselves, degraded and corrupted their ideals, dealing out harm instead of good to those around and below them.

The system, we have seen, defeated the noble individual, not by crushing or eliminating him (that happened only to stubborn, unyielding eccentrics like Olkhovsky), but by embracing him, converting him, swallowing him. It induced him to join its side — for most idealistic motives — and thereby made its conquest.

As we have moved from the Stalinist and near-Stalinist images of villains to those which the Party found more and more disturbing, a curious change took place in the stories we were looking at. The works became more and more similar to nineteenth-century Russian literature, to negative, critical realism, rather than to the optimistic socialist realism. This is a significant shift. It is further supported by the post-Stalinist authors' little touches of explicit comparison, here and there, between Soviet conditions and those of Tsarist Russia. Forty years after the Revolution, then, Russian writers were insinuating that the powers that be, the governmental authorities, again were playing the repressive role which they had traditionally played, in the intellectuals' opinion, before 1917. Again the writer is praising the lone hero who is going against the system; again he is revealing the iniquities of the rulers and of the social structure of the country. The writers find themselves in the curious position of implicitly calling for another revolution. Somewhere along the line, not only the lives of various individuals have gone off the right track, but the entire cause of the Revolution, conceived by some of its supporters in the spirit of liberty and human equality, dedicated to enabling man to develop to unprecedented heights, has somehow turned off in the wrong direction, so that the job has to be done all over again. As in nineteenth-century literature, the nonconformist and the outcast again stand for justice and humanity, the man in power for tyranny and dehumanization.

By what criteria do the authors who make the deepest analysis of the nature of villainy in Soviet life judge their characters? Their decisions appear to be based for the most part on traditional, liberal, humanistic values. Most Western thinkers, from Montaigne through Locke and Lincoln, could probably subscribe to them. Their ulti-

143

mate measure of the value of a system of social organization is its effects on the human individual: the kind of man it makes him. They wish man to be large, generous, unselfish, self-disciplined, free in his thinking, speaking, and acting. In fact the opposites of most of the qualities summarized here as the main traits of the Soviet literary villains yield a satisfactory composite portrait of the Russian intellectuals' ideal individual. Behind this ideal stands a tradition of Western humanism, with its stress on the free development of the self. In one feature only is there again perhaps exceptionally great emphasis among the Russian writers. Concern for the community and for the need to work for future generations appears more deeply ingrained in the Soviet writers' ideals than among most of their Western counterparts.

CHAPTER V

The Climax with DOCTOR ZHIVAGO

In 1954 foreign visitors to Russia who had personal friends among Soviet writers came back with very encouraging and almost unbelievable reports. The word was being passed around that Boris Pasternak was writing and would soon publish three works: an autobiography, a novel, and a collection of poetry.

This was surprising news for several reasons. First of all, Pasternak had been in great disfavor with the authorities. His poetry was lyrical, subjective, complex, and completely unrelated to the social themes of the day which the Party liked literature to treat. He consistently refused to obey the injunctions of socialist realism and was frequently attacked by official spokesmen. Since Zhdanov's onslaughts on literary dissidents in 1946, Pasternak's poetry had not been published in Russia. On the other hand, he continued to translate from foreign languages. Particularly his marvelously poetic, painstaking, and accurate translations of the major plays of Shakespeare made him famous in Russia. He translated also from Caucasian languages and from the German.

Pasternak, born in 1890, was intellectually formed by the best in prerevolutionary European thought. His parents were in touch with the most advanced thinkers of Central and Western Europe; he himself studied in Marburg under the philosopher Hermann Cohen. It was no wonder that in Stalinist Russia he was viewed as an alien. Unlike most of the Soviet writers, he is said never to have compromised even to the extent of writing one poem in praise of Stalin or on a Stalinist topic. The wonder was that he still continued to live at liberty. One explanation occasionally advanced in private by Russian authors was that Pasternak was regarded by officials (and

145

even by some of his friends) as something of a madman, who could be tolerated because of his harmlessness and because of the privileged, asylum-like shelter won for him by his position as a mystic or a holy lunatic. Party men may have been as indulgent toward Pasternak as one of Doctor Zhivago's interlocutors is toward him, when listening with a smile, he "took the doctor's words for the fooling of a witty eccentric."* To the wide public in Russia Pasternak was known only as a translator; to a narrower literary circle, as a nonconforming, excellent poet, perhaps the best Russian poet since Alexander Blok. His poems circulated in manuscript and were learned by heart by members of the literary intelligentsia and students. It came as a great surprise in 1954 to hear that cultural controls had relaxed to the point where Pasternak's own works, as distinguished from the safer translations in which he had taken refuge, could again be published.

The second reason for astonishment was that he was said to be writing a novel. Pasternak had written some prose in the past, but it was poetic, lyrical prose, nothing which would lead one to expect that he would turn to the composition of a novel. The reports about an autobiography also aroused much curiosity. Pasternak was unlikely to conceal or falsify his opinions. How could he write and publish in Russia what he truly thought of the last quarter of a century? And how would this autobiography differ from his earlier autobiographical *Safe Conduct* (1931)?

* There are also various speculations that Stalin protected Pasternak. Mikhail Koryakov suggests in the *New Review* (*Novy Zhurnal*), December 1958, that Stalin extended his protection to Pasternak because of a superstitious fear of the prophet-like powers of the poet and because of a cryptic note written by Pasternak on the occasion of the death of Stalin's wife Allilueva in November 1932. The *Literary Gazette* of November 17, 1932, printed a letter to Stalin signed by thirty-three Soviet writers. Following it was a note written by Pasternak, explaining that he had read the collective letter by the writers; instead of signing it, he wrote his own enigmatic text: "I join in the sentiments of my colleagues. On the eve, deeply and concentratedly, I thought about Stalin; as an artist, for the first time. In the morning I read the news. I was shaken as if I had been present, right there, as if I have lived and seen it. Boris Pasternak." Rumor has it that Stalin's wife committed suicide; according to others, Stalin killed her. In any event it is certain that Stalin was greatly shaken by her death. Whether Pasternak's note is a threat or an unmitigated condolence, we cannot tell; it reads strangely, as if it were meant to sound like the hint of a poetic seer.

The magazine *Banner* in April 1954 lent credence to the rumors. It printed ten poems by Pasternak with a note indicating that they were taken from a novel, the last chapter of which would probably be completed in the summer. A note by Pasternak described its hero as "Yuri Andreevich Zhivago, a doctor, a man of thought, questing, of creative and artistic bent, who dies in 1929." The anthology *Day of Poetry* in 1956 published two more poems by Pasternak.

It is now a matter of common knowledge that *Doctor Zhivago* was never published in Russia, and that the manuscript was sent by the author to an Italian publisher, Feltrinelli, who later refused to return it when Soviet authorities demanded that it be revised or withdrawn. The novel has since been published in Italian, French, English, and other translations, and the Russian version has also been issued in the West.

An autobiography, it turned out, had also really been written by Pasternak. Like the novel, it was not published in Russia, but appeared in a French translation in Paris in the summer of 1958 and later in other translations. Apparently it had been intended as a preface to the planned anthology of verse, of which nothing came, in or out of Russia.

The reception of *Doctor Zhivago* in the West was sensational, but Soviet Russia reacted quietly until an event which made it impossible to ignore the novel any longer: the award of the Nobel Prize to Pasternak in October 1958. But before we examine the Soviet reaction to the award, let us look at some of the main features of the book itself.

Doctor Zhivago is a novel into which Pasternak has poured his mature thoughts about the meaning of the experiences of his generation. It is the story of the adventures and many reflective conversations of Yuri Zhivago, of the three women in his life, as well as of a host of other characters, who include a partisan leader, a lawyer, and a group of railway workers, seen in flashes from 1903 to 1929, with particular emphasis on the years of the Revolution and Civil War and with an epilogue set at the time of World War II. We meet the characters in a variety of settings, in riches and in poverty, whirling with the winds of the Revolution. We skip from one brief scene to another, from one indelibly etched image to another. Primarily through the mind of Zhivago, the intellectual, poetic physician, but also through several other characters, Pasternak broods about the meaning of the Russian Revolution, about what is important in life, about the place of art and the significance of love and history. Nature is the most striking setting of the book. Far from being mere background, it is a rich, poetically rendered presence ever before us, placed into a vital relationship with the characters' fates.

Zhivago, the central character, is at first sympathetic with the aims of the revolutionaries. He holds no brief for the *ancien régime*, private property, and what he terms "the acquisitive passions" of capitalism. Later, however, he comes to consider the Bolshevik revolutionary movement to be misguided, tragically distorted, and harmful. He believes Marxist theories to be gross oversimplifications of the realities of life. He calls Utopian Communist doctrines "this childish harlequinade of immature fantasies, these schoolboy escapades," and deplores that men lost their confidence in the value of their own opinions: "People imagined that it was out of date to follow their own moral sense, that they must all sing in chorus and live by other people's notions, notions that were being crammed down everybody's throat." Specific comments are made on Soviet Russian history. A character who survives Zhivago says: "I think that collectivization was an erroneous and unsuccessful measure and that it was impossible to admit the error. To conceal the failure people had to be cured, by every means of terrorism, of the habit of thinking and judging for themselves, and forced to see what didn't exist, to assert the very opposite of what their eyes told them. This accounts for the unexampled cruelty of the Ezhov period, the promulgation of a constitution that was never meant to be applied, and the introduction of elections not founded on the principle of free choice." These condemnations of the Soviet government and atmosphere are more explicit and sharper than anything we have encountered in our previous examples of Soviet writing.

Pasternak does not hesitate to have Zhivago say, "Marxism is too uncontrolled to be a science. Sciences are more balanced. Is Marxism objective? I don't know a movement more self-centered and further removed from the facts than Marxism." But he does not militate against Marxism in order to replace it with another social or political movement. He appears to oppose all organized reforms, all schemes of "social betterment." "Reshaping life! People who can say that may have lived through a lot, but have never understood a thing about life—they have never felt its breath, its soul . . . they look on it as a lump of coarse raw material that needs to be processed by them, to be ennobled by their touch. But life is never a material, a substance. If you want to know, life is the principle of self-renewal, it is constantly renewing and remaking and changing and transfiguring itself, it is infinitely beyond your or my obtuse theories."

Here we have Pasternak's central belief from which all others are derived. Zhivago, whose name is cognate with the Russian words for "living" and "alive," believes in life in a sense which completely contradicts the bases of Marxist thought. Not five-year plans, not the creation of a society based on theoretical blueprints, but concrete life itself, experienced and thought about by the individual, is meaningful to him. "The riddle of life, the riddle of death, the enchantment of genius, the enchantment of unadorned beauty"— those are his highest values. Pasternak has written a novel which is political only in the sense of being antipolitical. Just as Tolstoy's *War and Peace* is a historical novel which puts forward the theory that history cannot be written and that the human mind deceives itself when it thinks that it is capable of understanding events of history, so *Doctor Zhivago* is a political and social novel which presents the thesis that the effort to impose new political and social forms on life is a basic misunderstanding of life.

A far-reaching individualism—more extreme than that of most individualists in the West—is Pasternak's own philosophy. Zhivago even writes a pamphlet on the "theory of individuality as the biological basis of the organism." Thinking about life, the perception of aesthetic experience, and the understanding of history are the highest activities of which man is capable, in his opinion. To him the great contribution of Christianity is that the Gospels teach that "in that new way of living born of the heart, and in the new form of society, which is called the Kingdom of Heaven, there are no nations, there are only individuals."

Zhivago lives according to his theories of individualism. He opposes the Soviet system but does not struggle against it. His destruction is the tragedy of a passive victim; it is a parable of the destruction of the Russian intellectuals.

In *War and Peace* Tolstoy opposed to the delusions of self-important statesmen and historians the private life of two couples, Princess Mary and Nicholas, Natasha and Pierre. Family life in the second epilogue is triumphant over political life. Pasternak goes still further in the direction of individualism: political life is replaced not by family life but by the life of the individual. The greatest love of the book is not married love. Zhivago's highest union with another human being comes during his stay with Lara in the country, a scene which impressed several critics as one of the best of the entire novel. The love of Zhivago and Lara is a fulfillment through the communion of two individuals, not through the family unit. Lara and Zhivago later separate. Pasternak is careful to avoid Tolstoy's exaltation of the family. Tolstoy disintegrated the "collective" into molecules; Pasternak goes beyond him to a division into atoms, but atoms capable of a sense of communion with each other, as well as with history and with beauty.

In addition to his exultant and wise eulogy of human love, Pasternak expresses his admiration for art ("art always serves beauty, and beauty is delight in form, and form is the key to organic life, since no living thing can exist without it") and for an understanding of the processes of history (to him the antithesis to the state of nature is the state of history, as it was to Hegel — perhaps a trace of the influence of Pasternak's Hegelian teacher in Marburg, Hermann Cohen — in contradistinction to the Christian antithesis of the state of nature and the state of grace).

The dominant mood of the book combines sad resignation with a wonder at life's mysteries. One is aware throughout that this is not only a philosopher's, but also a painter's and a poet's novel. A painter's, because it leaps from one visually conceived image to another. A poet's, because its logic and system of connections rely on symbolic rather than the conventional narrative continuities of prose fiction. An insistent symbolism is basic to the book.

Yet there are passages in *Doctor Zhivago* which betray that though this is the work of a man in his fifties and sixties, it is clearly the author's first novel. Some transitions are clumsy and tenuous, the handling of dialogue slovenly. The reader occasionally loses track of who is talking to whom. The beginning of the book overwhelms one with too many underdeveloped characters, in too many brief scenes; the end is shadowy, schematic, perhaps even unfinished. It is clear that the author is contemptuous of what other novelists consider correctness, and is so impatient to speak about what to him are the important things that he jumps over all trivial matter. When he wants to move to a new dialogue or scene, he does so in a few bold, brief sentences, ignoring continuity, point of view, and probability. Yet the blemishes in this novel are not weighty enough to detract from its major effects. It is artistically superior to any of the other books discussed in this study, perhaps superior to any book written in Russia in the last quarter of a century. It surpasses all of them as a human and cultural document.

From the foregoing discussion it is clear that *Doctor Zhivago* confirms and carries even further our earlier findings about the Soviet authors' views of love and human villainy. To Pasternak, also, love is one of the main forces which make our lives human. He opposes it to the dehumanizing, mechanical, collective tendencies of Soviet Russia — for that matter, of all countries. Human villainy in its worst form is in his novel represented by men not unlike the villains we have analyzed earlier. Some of Pasternak's accounts of Pasha Antipov resemble the villains of Dudintsev, Kaverin, and Yashin, except that Pasternak is depicting at its earlier stage a process which the other authors represent in its maturity. Pasternak draws a portrait of the idealist beginning to be dehumanized by the Communist ideology in which he believes and by which he regulates his life, during the times of the Civil War, whereas the other authors represent the dehumanization of men of the 1940's and 1950's. Thus Lara in *Doctor Zhivago* sees Antipov, who is then a guerrilla leader under the pseudonym Strelnikov, in this manner: "It was as if something abstract had crept into his face and made it colorless. As if a living human face had become the embodiment of a principle, the image of an idea. My heart sank when I noticed it. I realized that this had happened to him because he had handed himself over to a superior force, but a force that is deadening and pitiless and will not spare him in the end."

Pasternak's autobiography, like that of any great poet and novelist, was bound to arouse considerable interest. What would the writer say about his own works? What light would the book throw on his mental processes, on his perception of the world around him? Would it provide new clues to the interpretation of his works?

In addition to answering such questions, Pasternak's brief autobiography also sparks immediate interest because of its author's position as a beleaguered, one-man fortress standing against official Soviet ideology within the USSR itself. As the author of a novel which challenged a political colossus, he is a man who, if not a martyr, surely has demonstrated his willingness to undergo martyrdom. *I Remember* continues his proud, dignified struggle. In his own name this time (not, as in *Zhivago,* in the name of a fictional protagonist, a thin enough disguise even in the novel), he contradicts many Soviet dogmas. Throughout, he denies that the artist should accept a public, social role. He says of the poet Vladimir Mayakovsky, "I could not understand his propagandist zeal . . . his complete subordination to the demand for topical subjects." For himself, he says, he has wanted a life of personal, private creation, following the dictates of his talent not the "social command" of the Party. "Life without privacy and without obscurity, life reflected in the splendor of a plate-glass show case is inconceivable to me," he writes, again in connection with a contrast he draws between his own literary career and that of Mayakovsky after 1917.

Pasternak deplores what Soviet propaganda has extolled, Mayakovsky's "preoccupation with the national balance sheet and the tragedy of the Supreme Council of National Economy." What the Party and Mayakovsky (at least some of the time) considered an exemplary devotion and a proper consecration of poetic gifts to the demands of society, Pasternak calls "a straying away from the true and sincere path." He ridicules two famous statements made by Stalin in the early 1930's: that life in Russia had become "easier and more cheerful," and that Mayakovsky was the best and most talented poet of the epoch.

The majority of the poets he praises most highly are those who suffered under the Soviet regime. Some of them have recently been halfheartedly rehabilitated, some are still unwelcome in the official hall of fame: Tsvetaeva (who killed herself after returning to Russia from exile in the West), Annensky (a symbolist), Akhmatova (repeatedly a victim of attacks), Aseev, Bely. Of Mayakovsky, Pasternak now says he likes best not the officially eulogized later poems, but the early, lyrical poetry, which was futuristic and is being half ignored and half apologized for by Soviet critics. Pasternak even makes the broad statement that the last years of Mayakovsky's life (the late 1920's, the period praised in Stalin's slogan) were a time when "all poetry had ceased to exist" and "literature had stopped."

But we must not think Pasternak is bold only in his judgment of the works of others. He is equally sweeping and critical in speaking of his own. He condemns brusquely many of his earlier works; he makes it clear that a sharp change occurred in his own literary taste. Of all his works, he says in one passage, *Zhivago* is the only one of which he is not ashamed. Pasternak's autobiography deserves to be thought of in connection with the aging Tolstoy's repudiation of his earlier works, Gogol's change of heart, and Chaucer's recantation, even though it is not so extreme as those three writers' revulsion against their own earlier creations had been.

The personal parts of the sketch end with the Revolution, just as his autobiographical *Safe Conduct* (1931) had. Pasternak explains the difficulties of writing about the Soviet period and the "new trials with which this world confronts the human personality and man's honor, pride, and endurance. . . . One would have to write about it in a way to make the heart stop beating and the hair stand on end. To write about it in an ordinary and commonplace way, to write about it unemotionally, to write about it less colorfully than Gogol

153

and Dostoevsky have depicted Petersburg, is not only senseless and useless; to write like that would be both dishonest and base. We are far from that ideal." His readers would add at this point that *Doctor Zhivago* is an attempt to write, not dishonestly and not basely, but truthfully and vividly, about the Revolution and Soviet Russia.

In the purely subjective sections of the autobiography Pasternak gives sharply focused moments of recollection: a night when as a child he awoke, cried, listened to music, was comforted by his mother, and caught a glimpse of Leo Tolstoy; various passing experiences and encounters, outstanding because of what they meant to him emotionally or because of his way of describing them, a poet's way, as in the simile, "Like the front of a cart on its coupling-pole, the night on high slowly turned the whole body of its starry chariot," or his rich description of a coachman's inn in a forest, visited after a ride in a *kibitka*.

This is the autobiography of a sensitive man, who is also a man of great pride, nobility, and uncompromising honesty. We feel in him a strange combination of one who watches the world from a great height, detached, yet is flooded by emotion through the direct impact of many details of what he sees.

After the announcement of October 23, 1958, that the Nobel Prize had been given to Pasternak, Soviet authorities preserved silence for a couple of days and then opened an attack against him which served to draw the whole world's attention to his fate. He was called a Judas, a traitor, and a helper of the capitalists, and, as is now generally known, only his letters of explanation and apology (dated October 31 and November 5) saved him from being arrested or exiled. Within Russia, only a relatively small number of persons, it may be presumed, had had the opportunity to read *Doctor Zhivago* — a few high officials, and those who read Russian or translated copies secretly brought into the country. The general literary public was exposed to months of vilification of the novel and its author, without having had an opportunity to read the work itself.

The most complete account of the book available to the Soviet reader was contained in two documents printed in the *Literary Ga-*

zette of October 25, 1958. One was a vehement attack in an article three columns long, written after the Nobel Prize award, calling the novel a "counterrevolutionary, slanderous work," and blaming Pasternak for "having found it possible to turn over the manuscript of *Doctor Zhivago* to bourgeois publishers" after it had been rejected by "the editorial boards of Soviet magazines and publishers." This article refers to the autobiography as well as the novel, calls Pasternak a "megalomaniac," and declares he chose "the road of shame and dishonor."

The other was a much longer document occupying three pages of the newspaper. Ostensibly it was a letter of rejection of the book dated September 1956 and signed by five members of the editorial board of *New World*. This letter is written in more moderate language. It is doubtful, however, whether it is the original letter composed in 1956. Many extensive quotations from the novel are included in it, the presence of which would not make sense in a letter of rejection addressed to the author and enclosing the manuscript being returned — surely the author would be expected to understand the references without any extended quotations. Evidently, then, at least these quotations (and possibly other sections) were added in 1958 for the benefit of the readers of the newspaper.

The letter analyzes at great length the themes of *Doctor Zhivago*. It stresses the title character's "individualism hypertrophied to improbable size." The editors say to Pasternak: "In your opinion Doctor Zhivago is the peak of the Russian intelligentsia. In our opinion he is its cesspool." They quote many anti-Marxist passages from the book; they deplore the fact that the characters of the book do not define their attitudes to such historical events as the overthrow of the Tsar, Kerensky's assumption of power, Kornilov's revolt, the dispersal of the Constitutional Assembly; they blame Pasternak for failing to distinguish between the February and October revolutions. They cite many passages attacking what in the English translation is rather flatteringly called "gregariousness" (in the Russian original, *stadnost,* close to "herd instinct"). There are no adequate opponents to Zhivago in the book, the editors conclude.

155

Zhivago must be taken as the mouthpiece for the author, and his views as hostile to the Revolution and to the Soviet system.

The quotations from the book are interestingly enough for the most part the same as those which Western critics have used (including those cited in this chapter). The editors' letter is on the whole a fair and truthful summary of the book. Zhivago is indeed the spokesman for Pasternak's viewpoint, and he is anti-Soviet and anti-Marxist, as we have seen earlier. The letter is not entirely accurate, however. In several details Pasternak might well claim to have been misrepresented, as when the editors incorrectly stress the material worries and the desire for comfort of some of the characters or dwell on Zhivago's vanity and ignore proofs of his altruism. But in general, on the most important issues, the letter does not summarize the book in terms that differ markedly from those of its admirers abroad. It disagrees with Western opinion in one most important regard, of course: it takes for granted that if the book expresses anti-Soviet sentiments, then without further argument it cannot be published.

Doctor Zhivago and Pasternak's autobiography have an anomalous position within Soviet Russian literature. Having been published only abroad, they cannot be considered to belong to Soviet Russian literature in exactly the same way in which *Not by Bread Alone* and *Home Town,* for example, do form part of it. On the other hand Pasternak's works cannot be assigned to the voluminous Russian *émigré* literature, either: Boris Pasternak has lived and is living inside Soviet Russia. (There are several partial analogues to the fate of *Doctor Zhivago*; Zamyatin's *We,* for instance, was written by its author inside Russia, but published only outside of the country, in New York in 1924 and in Prague in 1927.)

Several considerations, it seems to me, compel us to include *Doctor Zhivago* in any examination of Soviet Russian literature of the 1950's. In the first place, after Pasternak was awarded the Nobel Prize, such a turmoil was aroused over *Doctor Zhivago* in the Soviet press, in public meetings, and in private discussions among writers and other Soviet citizens interested in literature that by virtue of that fact alone the book became an integral part of Soviet literary life of the period.

Secondly, as we have seen, Pasternak carries to the extreme some of the themes which other Soviet authors have treated more moderately or gingerly. A consideration of *Doctor Zhivago* is, then, necessary in order to complete the picture.

Finally there is the fact that an ever-increasing number of Russians inside the USSR have found access to the text of the novel and have read it. Copies of the novel were distributed to Russian visitors at the World's Fair in Brussels; a few privileged, highly placed persons read the book in manuscript after Pasternak submitted it for publication in 1956, and through a variety of channels, a steady trickle of copies is finding its way into the Soviet Union in Russian as well as French, English, and Italian. Every copy available is read and re-read by many readers. It is safe to assume that within a decade, even if the novel should never be printed inside Russia, it will have achieved a substantial circulation and won a reading public which will make its influence a solid fact. From an even longer perspective, I should not hesitate to hazard the prophecy that when Soviet Russian literature of the 1950's is discussed thirty or fifty years from now, *Doctor Zhivago* will seem such a central, overshadowingly outstanding book of the period that its omission from the rolls of that body of literature on the grounds that it was printed abroad and not inside the USSR would appear entirely absurd.

The suppression of *Doctor Zhivago* in Russia is not as surprising as the publication of poems from it in 1954 and the apparent intention at that time to publish the whole novel. Even at the height of the interval of freedom, its publication in Russia in unrevised form would have been unthinkable. The violence of the onslaught on Pasternak after October 25, 1958, is explainable by the new line toward literature which was then being tightened by the Party authorities. Failure to clarify the Party's stand on *Doctor Zhivago* would have been inconsistent with the severity of the Party pronouncements on literature on the eve of the First Russian Writers' Union Congress (held in December 1958) and the Third USSR Writers' Congress, then being prepared for 1959.

In the summer of 1959, some moderately conciliatory gestures were made by Soviet officials toward Pasternak. Threats against him and abuse in the press dwindled and then at least temporarily ceased. But the outside world still remembered how the resources of terror of a totalitarian state had been marshaled to crush one solitary writer in the fall of 1958.

CHAPTER VI

The Interval IN PERSPECTIVE

THE INNOVATIONS made by some of the Soviet Russian authors in the years 1954-1957 were limited to themes and attitudes toward their subjects. They made little attempt to escape the confines of socialist realism in style or manner. Most of the dissident authors wrote with the same reverence for fact, for the clearly, simply, conventionally presented scene and character, as such officially approved authors as Simonov and Fedin. In literary technique there has been no return to the 1920's, no revival of the symbolism of an Olesha, the modernism of a Pilnyak, the Maupassantesque precision and *mot juste* of an Isaac Babel. In 1958 as in 1952, it was still true that Joyce, Proust, Kafka, and Freud might as well never have existed for all the influence they exerted on Soviet writing.

Another dogma which was not challenged in Russia was the primacy of Party leadership in culture. Authors dared to disagree on the direction in which the Party leaders should steer literature; but they did not suggest — as Trotsky urged in the early 1920's — that literature may be regarded as a sphere of legitimately autonomous endeavor in which the Party should refrain from active guidance.

The day is still far off when it will be rewarding to discuss Soviet writing in purely literary terms. The recent works which have aroused the most violent controversy did so for nonliterary reasons, through their social, political, and philosophical content. They are not artistically worthless, but their extra-literary interest predominates over the literary. Only a few exceptions exist to this generalization: *Doctor Zhivago,* the poems of Shchipachev and Martynov, which show a truly lyrical note and considerable formal originality,

159

a few short stories penetrating in characterization, and parts of some other novels.

We should err if we considered all or even most of the works cited to have been composed by authors eager to repudiate the Communist Party or consciously hostile to the principles and foundations of the Soviet Russian state. Probably very few of them, possibly only Boris Pasternak, consider the Soviet state basically mistaken and wrong. Hostility to the Party, on the other hand, is probably felt by a greater number of them, just as it is by a good many Soviet citizens in other occupations. But one can find much wrong with one's country and the Party in exclusive control of it and still consider oneself a loyal or even a devoted citizen.

On the other hand, many of the ideas expressed in the Soviet writings may jointly form a more formidable indictment of the state of affairs in Russia than the writers themselves realize. It is quite possible to be unaware of the full implications of one's own specific observations and opinions. When they are put together with those made by others, as has been done in this study, they may constitute a coherent body of opinions which taken as a whole is far more incompatible with the official state and Party doctrines than the individual statements are.

We should overestimate the significance of the writers' "rebellion" if we regarded it as proof of the readiness of Soviet intellectuals to take overt action against their government. The word "rebellion" itself may be misleading in this context. We must also guard against exaggerating the degree of freedom actually granted to the writers in the years 1954-1957. On the other hand, we should be equally wrong if we discounted the writers' dissident opinions merely because the writers may not have explicitly formulated in their own minds the implications of their ideas.

Several facts emerge from our examination of the thematic content of Soviet literature.

Many Soviet authors tacitly or overtly take for granted that social stratification exists in the USSR. They do not attempt to pay lip-service to the official view that in the "socialistic" stage of development no classes like those of the capitalistic world exist, only social groupings of friendly workers, peasants, and intellectuals. Soviet literature of the past few years presents a picture of a class of rulers, of an elite, who live a far different life from the ruled and are isolated socially and personally from the masses of the population.

The outlook of this upper class is very different from that of the lower class. The hardships of the workers and peasants are known to the rulers only from the vantage point of their city office desk. The elite hold a rosy view of Soviet life, but when they are brought into contact with concrete facts, they become confused and flee to the security of their office shelter.

Some members of the elite commit transgressions of varying degrees of seriousness: most venial, resorting to clichés instead of facing a problem, refusing to produce a new machine or permit a new drug to be developed; more serious, neglect of workers' living conditions; most criminal, sending an opponent to years of forced labor on false charges.

The offenses of the elite are not depicted as results of their innate sinfulness or as "survivals of capitalism," but as explainable by the mechanisms of the Soviet system itself. The "contradictions" are built in. They are fundamental, multiform, pervasive, and serious in their consequences.

Some of the Soviet writers, permitted during the "thaw" to indulge in freer criticism than under Stalin, have gone beyond the limits which the government assumed they would observe. They have not restricted themselves to exposing a few isolated bureaucrats; consciously or unconsciously, often perhaps without realizing the implications of what they were saying, they have pointed a finger at the root, not merely the excrescence, of the evil. Paradoxically the writers are often applying the sociological method of class analysis, almost Marxist in its exploiter-versus-worker groupings, against the state which purports to be an embodiment of Marxist ideas.

Khrushchev's attacks on Stalin have tended to isolate Stalinism as a phenomenon unrelated to other aspects of Soviet life. He has preserved silence about two serious questions arising out of his indictment of Stalin: how it was possible for Stalinism to develop in Soviet society (is there anything in the society which permitted, perhaps even encouraged, the emergence of Stalinism?) and whether it did not have consequences beyond itself (did it not taint other areas of Soviet life?). Soviet writers have gone beyond Khrushchev; they have answered both questions, at least by implication. Their books show mechanisms in Soviet society which favor lesser men of Stalin's kind. Hence the many "contradictions" between the thousands of little Stalins helped upward by various institutions (or not prevented from rising by any institutionalized checks) and the masses of the population. Stalinism pervaded life; it was not an isolated phenomenon which could neatly be excised all by itself.

Milovan Djilas in *The New Class* had the courage to write of the rise of a new ruling class and Communist bureaucracy in Yugoslavia and of the conflict between them and the people. Applying a Marxist analysis of society to the supposedly new Yugoslavia (and commenting on East European conditions in general), he found that far from being classless and equalitarian, the countries under Communist rule had merely replaced one set of rulers by another. The old exploiters had been expropriated, but the men in possession of the economy, this time not through personal ownership of it but through their power over the Party, the instrument of economic and social control, constituted a new class of rulers, with its own vested interests and prerogatives. In the works of Soviet novelists and playwrights, we have found data pointing in the same direction.

On the positive side, Soviet writers constitute a resurgence of humanism. They are united in condemning the many forms of degradation of man which they have witnessed in Russian life around them. In this respect not only *Doctor Zhivago* and *Not by Bread Alone,* but Soviet literature of the years 1954-1957 taken collectively is a document of particularly great historical significance. It shows that after decades of Stalinism, the desire for human values flaunted by the country's system had not disappeared; it had not even diminished. Outward signs of it had not been permitted for years. One might have thought it had been extirpated. Yet at the first opportunity that came, with Stalin's death, this desire expressed itself. It had lived an underground existence. After 1953, it flared up openly again.

162

The humanistic aspirations of the Soviet writers form the core from which emanate all their criticisms of Soviet conditions of life and the demands for improvements which they make implicitly or explicitly. They are asking for reverence for Man. Fundamentally, they are all moralists. They want the truth to be told, to all the people, and the ubiquitous lying to cease. They resent deeply the distortion and withholding of facts, the false communiqués, the "varnishing of reality"; they deplore the failure to trust the people which is behind the careful suppression of information and the selection of a fare of lies and half-truths for their consumption.

The outraged sense of insult at being kept from dangerous contacts with truth is clear in the pages of almost all the works we have looked at. A brief expression of it is present in V. Goncharov's poem "I Hate," published in 1956, which uses a photographer-retoucher as its vehicle to attack Stalinist lying:

> I hate the retouchers.
> There is no work
> More terrible than their work:
> For money they rid the world
> Of the truth.
> A boy is crying,
> But the artful scalpel
> Always does its job
> And this boy right away
> Will be smiling
> To please the world.
>
> . . . . . .
>
> Here is the dull face
> Of a murderer and scoundrel.
> Take the scalpel —
> And the portrait
> Presents a kindly fellow.
> I hate the retouchers
> Of the everyday world.
> They are ready to put a mask
> All over our planet.
>
> . . . .
>
> Our planet is dearer to us
> Without extra prettifications.

163

> No matter how you retouch it
> The earth will be the earth.
> You know what is true.
> Like your heart
> The truth is always with you.

The Soviet writers are asking for dignity and individual rights and at times for what we should call civil liberties. Their demands really constitute a proposal for a Soviet version of a Bill of Rights. They are condemning a series of injustices: dismissals of workers for insufficient or illegitimate reasons, persecutions of Jews and of those who happen to have relatives or friends abroad, abuses of the judicial system, tyrannical practices within the Communist Party, secret police methods. As Yashin expressed it in his story, human beings ought to be treated like human beings, not like "levers."

Great moral zeal is a trait shared by all the Soviet writers. Their books aim at a moral revolution in their readers. The writers burn with the desire to make people become better beings and in turn to inspire them with the zeal to reform others. The books are full of fervor based on love for a variety of objects: work and hard effort; industrial and scientific progress; Russia; the welfare of the people of the country; peace; the future generations. Their authors would evidently have understood — and been understood by — the fervent writers of New England in the period of its flowering and the Russian reformers and some of the revolutionaries of the last century. This rather old-fashioned, eager, touchingly uncynical, unskeptical, nineteenth-century idealism of the Soviet authors is one of their most surprising characteristics.

It is encouraging that after forty years of Soviet rule, the Russian intellectuals have not departed widely from Western traditional humanistic ideals.

In a few respects, however, their attitudes do differ from prevailing American attitudes. Their view of property, of ownership of material things, is more negative than ours. It is difficult to say whether the cause of this is the influence of the traditions of nineteenth-century Russian revolutionary ideals or of the socialistic ideology of Soviet Russia. Most likely several influences are at work. Soviet writers are quite antimaterialistic in regard to the owning of summer houses, cars, furniture, apartments. To desire such things is to them a sign of one's moral weakness. Far from judging the possession of wealth, good clothes, and television sets to be signs of success or of the superior worth of a person, they tend to consider them indications of the person's corruption. Soviet writers have a strong bias toward admiring poverty, suspecting riches. This bias against materialistic and bourgeois and in favor of ascetic, underdog, and proletarian values, which used to be directed against the nineteenth-century *meshchane,* aristocrats, and capitalists of Tsarist Russia, is now aimed against the social elite of Soviet Russia, the Drozdovs and Kramovs.

The widest gap between Russia and the West is the Soviet writers' feeling for the group. The Soviet author, as we saw earlier, does want certain rights of the individual to be safeguarded. But this does not prevent him from adhering at the same time to a national, social feeling which is collectivistic rather than individualistic in nature. Even the most critical anti-Stalinist writers share this earnest, dedicated sense of the linking of people together in a communal effort (except Pasternak, the most individualistic of them all, who retains a feeling for the sharing of a common humanity, but repudiates social, organized undertakings). In Western novels one frequently sees a conglomeration of individuals interested in living their own lives and thinking largely of themselves or their families. The Soviet novelists for the most part present as their spokesmen characters who aspire at participating in some larger undertaking. This may be an effort quite different from the officially set, propagandized aims of the Communist Party. It is usually some idealistic cause which transcends the individual's personal life, encompassing wide reaches of society or the remote future. It gives the individual a sense of purpose, and of participation in an altruistic undertaking.

There are many things to which the Soviet novelist is blind and which he could learn from the West. Most significant for the political fortunes of the Russian people is his failure to realize that moral exhortation and reform alone are not enough, that institutional machinery must be provided if individual rights are to be recognized and protected. The Russians are prone to stop at the moment of having enunciated a fine general moral principle, as if with its formulation the whole task were accomplished. They seem to see no need for proceeding to a practical implementation, to an actual program based on the noble principle. They fail to realize that institutions and social checks and balances must exist if human rights are to move from the realm of the abstract into the concrete world of everyday life.

On the other hand, we in the West could learn a great deal from the Russians. We have lost much of their youthful spirit of idealism. Sometimes we find ourselves swamped in materialistic pursuits which the Russian writers would consider selfish and degrading. Most important of all, often we live lives isolated from other people, lacking in a sense of common purpose which would provide us with long-range goals toward which to work and orient our lives. We could well allow ourselves to be inspired by the Russian intellectuals' greater social sense of responsibility, as well as by their contempt for the frivolities of life.

Russian literature, then, points not only to the weaknesses — sometimes catastrophical ones — of Soviet life. It also reveals some of the elements of Russia's strength.

Bibliography and Index

BIBLIOGRAPHY

M o s t of the important Soviet novels (as was the practice in prerevolutionary Russia) are first published serially, in one of the several monthly magazines, and only later issued in a separate book edition, sometimes in a revised version. The most important magazines are *Novy Mir* (*New World*), which enjoys the privilege of having the greatest number of pages per issue, *Oktyabr* (*October*), *Znamya* (*Banner*), *Zvezda* (*Star*), *Teatr* (*Theater*), and the more recently established *Neva* and *Moskva* (*Moscow*). All are official organs of the Union of Writers, except for *Theater*, which is the organ jointly of the Union of Writers and the Ministry of Culture. *Neva* is the organ of the Russian Republic Union together with the Leningrad Union; *Moscow* of the Russian Republic Union together with the Moscow Union; the others of the USSR Union of Writers. *Banner, October, New World, Theater,* and *Moscow* are published in Moscow; *Neva* and *Star* in Leningrad.

Aleshin, S. *Alone* (*Odna*), *Teatr*, August 1956.

Alexandrova, Vera. "Forty Years of Soviet Literature" ("K sorokaletiyu sovetskoi literatury"), *Novy Zhurnal*, December 1957.

———. "Soviet Literature after the Twentieth Congress of the Communist Party" ("Sovetskaya literatura posle XX sezda KPSS"), *Novy Zhurnal*, September 1956.

———. Monthly articles on Russian Literature in *Sotsialistichesky Vestnik*.

Aliger, Margarita. "Conversation with a Friend" ("Razgovor s drugom"), *Znamya*, June 1954.

———. Recantation, *Literaturnaya Gazeta*, October 8, 1957.

Ashby, Eric. *Scientist in Russia*. New York: Penguin Books, 1947.

Bek, Alexander. *The Life of Berezhkov* (*Zhizn Berezhkova*), *Novy Mir*, January–March 1956.

Berggolts, Olga. "The Answer" ("Otvet"), *Novy Mir*, August 1956.

———. "Conversation about Lyrical Poetry" ("Razgovor o lirike"), *Literaturnaya Gazeta*, April 16, 1953.

Crankshaw, Edward. *Russia without Stalin*. New York: Viking Press, 1956.

Current Digest of the Soviet Press. Contains many reports of Soviet articles about literature.

Dar, D. *Good Luck! A Tale about Konstantine Tsiolkovsky* (*V dobry chas! Povest o Konstantine Tsiolkovskom*). Moscow, 1948.

The Day of Poetry (*Den poezii*). Moscow, 1956.

Djilas, Milovan. *The New Class*. New York: Frederick A. Praeger, 1957.

Dudintsev, Vladimir. *Not by Bread Alone* (*Ne khlebom edinym*), *Novy Mir*, August–October 1956. American edition, New York: Dutton and Co., 1957.

169

Ehrenburg, Ilya. "The Lessons of Stendhal" ("Uroki Stendalya"), *Inostrannaya literatura*, June 1957.

———. "The Poetry of Marina Tsvetaeva" ("Poeziya Mariny Tsvetaevoy"), *Literaturnaya Moskva*, II, Moscow, 1956.

———. *The Thaw (Ottepel)*, Part I, *Znamya*, May 1954; Part II, *Znamya*, April 1956. American edition of Part I only, *The Thaw*. Chicago: Regnery, 1955.

———. "The Work of a Writer" ("O rabote pisatelya"), *Znamya*, October 1953.

Elsberg, Ya. "Unjustified Haughtiness" ("Neopravdannoe vysokomerie"), *Literaturnaya Gazeta*, June 13, 1957.

Evtushenko, E. "Station Winter" ("Stantsiya Zima"), *Oktyabr*, October 1956, pp. 26–47.

"First Steps to a New Russian Literature," *Times Literary Supplement*, August 16, 1957, pp. ii–iii.

Friedberg, Maurice. "New Editions of Soviet *Belles-Lettres*," *American Slavic and East European Review*, February 1954, pp. 72–88.

Goncharov, V. "I Hate" ("Ya nenavizhu"), *Den poezii*. Moscow, 1956.

Gor, Gennadi. "The Real Hero of Artistic Books about Science" ("O podlinnom geroe nauchno-khudozhestvennykh knig"), *Neva*, September 1956.

Gorbunov, Nikolai. "The Mistake (A Monologue of a Professor)," ("Oshibka (Monolog professora)"), *Nash Sovremennik*, Spring 1957.

Granin, Daniel. "Personal Convictions" ("Sobstvennoe mnenie"), *Novy Mir*, August 1956. Trans. by Valentin Eyre under the title "A Personal Opinion," in *Bitter Harvest*, ed. by Edmund Stillman. New York: Frederick A. Praeger, 1959.

———. *Those Who Seek (Iskateli)*. Leningrad, 1955.

Kaverin, Venyamin. *Searches and Hopes (Poiski i nadezhdy)*, *Literaturnaya Moskva*, II. Moscow, 1956.

Kirsanov, Semen. "The Seven Days of the Week" ("Sem dnei nedeli"), *Novy Mir*, September 1956.

Kochetov, Vsevolod. *The Ershov Brothers (Bratya Ershovy)*, *Neva*, June–July 1958.

Korneichuk, Alexander. *The Wings (Krylya)*, *Novy Mir*, November 1954.

Koryakov, Mikhail. "Russia's Thermometer" ("Termometr Rossii"), *Novy Zhurnal*, December 1958.

Kron, A. "A Writer's Notes" ("Zametki pisatelya"), *Literaturnaya Moskva*, II. Moscow, 1956.

Lenoble, G. "A New Stage: Reading and Reflecting on 'Battle on the Way'" ("Na novom etape: chitaya i obdumyvaya 'Bitvu v puti'"), *Voprosy Literatury*, July 1959.

Leonov, Leonid. *The Russian Forest (Russky les)*. Moscow, 1953.

Lvov, B. "A Farce or an Elegy" ("Fars ili elegiya"), *Teatr*, July 1957.

Lvova, Kseniya. *Elena*, in *Almanakh: God Tridtsat Vosmoy*, XIX, 1955, Book I, pp. 70–235.

Markhasev, L. "The Costs of the Middle Level!" ("Izderzhki 'srednego urovnya'!"), *Teatr*, October 1956.

Mathewson, Rufus W. Jr. *The Positive Hero in Russian Literature*. New York: Columbia University Press, 1958.

Matlock, J. F., Jr. "Russia's Literary Softening," *Saturday Review*, February 2, 1957, pp. 9–11, 35–36.

Monas, Sidney. "A Miracle Is a Miracle" (review of *Doctor Zhivago*), *Hudson Review*, Winter 1958–1959, pp. 612–619.

Nekrasov, Viktor. *Home Town* (*V rodnom gorode*), *Novy Mir*, October–November 1954. French edition, *La ville natale*. Paris: Les Editeurs Français Réunis, 1957.

Nikolaeva, Galina. *A Battle on the Way* (*Bitva v puti*), *Oktyabr*, March, May, and July 1957. Also revised in a book edition, Moscow, 1958.

Nilin, Pavel. *Cruelty* (*Zhestokost*), *Znamya*, November–December 1956. American edition, *Comrade Venka*. New York: Simon and Schuster, 1959.

Ostrovsky, Nikolai. *How the Steel Is Tempered* (*Kak zakalyalas shtal*). Moscow, 1934. English edition, London: Secker and Warburg, 1937.

Ovechkin, Valentin. "Initiative and Talents" ("Ob initsiative i talantakh"), *Novy Mir*, January 1956.

Panova, Vera. *Kruzhilikha*, *Znamya*, November–December 1947. English edition, *The Factory*. London: Putnam, 1949.

———. *The Seasons of the Year* (*Vremena goda*), *Novy Mir*, November–December 1953. English edition, *Span of the Year*. London: Harvill Press, 1957.

Paperny, Z. *Genya and Senya* (*Genya i Senya*), *Teatr*, August 1956.

Pasternak, Boris. *Doctor Zhivago*. New York: Pantheon, 1958. Russian edition, Ann Arbor, Mich.: University of Michigan Press, 1959.

———. *Essai d'Autobiographie*. Paris, 1959. American edition, *I Remember: Sketch for an Autobiography*. New York: Pantheon, 1959.

———. "Poems from the Novel in Prose 'Doctor Zhivago'" ("Stikhi iz romana v proze 'Doktor Zhivago'"), *Znamya*, April 1954.

Pilnyak, Boris. "The Law of the Wolf," in *Azure Cities: Stories of New Russia*. New York: International Publishers, 1929.

Pogodin, Nikolai. *Petrarch's Sonnet* (*Sonet Petrarki*), *Literaturnaya Moskva*, II. Moscow, 1956.

Pomerantsev, Vladimir. "On Sincerity in Literature" ("Ob iskrennosti v literature"), *Novy Mir*, December 1953.

Rozhdestvenny, R. "My Love" ("Moya lyubov"), *Oktyabr*, January 1955.

Sevak, Paruir. "Uneasy Conversation" ("Nelegky razgovor"), *Novy Mir*, June 1956.

Shtein, Alexander. *A Personal Case* (*Personalnoe delo*), *Pesy*. Moscow, 1956.

Shundik, N. "The Writer Is Responsible to the People" ("Pisatel otvetstvenen pered narodom"), *Neva*, October 1957.

Simmons, Ernest J. *Russian Fiction and Soviet Ideology: Introduction to Fedin, Leonov, and Sholokhov*. New York: Columbia University Press, 1958.

———. "Soviet Literature, 1950–1955," *Annals of the American Academy of Political and Social Science*, January 1956, pp. 89–103.

Slonim, Marc. *Modern Russian Literature: From Chekhov to the Present*. New York: Oxford University Press, 1953.

———. "Pasternak's Novel" ("Roman Pasternaka"), *Novy Zhurnal*, March 1958.

Stackelberg, G. A. von, "Socialist Realism after the Twentieth Party Congress," *Bulletin: Institute for the Study of the USSR*, March 1957, pp. 13–22.

"The State of Soviet Literature," *Times Literary Supplement*, August 5, 1955, pp. xxxii–xxxiii.

Struve, Gleb. *Geschichte der Sowjetliteratur*. Munich: Isar Verlag, 1958.

171

――――. "Russia Five Years after Stalin: Literature," *New Leader*, April 7, 1958, pp. 16–21.

――――. "Soviet Literature after De-Stalinization," *Bulletin: Institute for the Study of the USSR*, May 1957, pp. 27–34.

――――. *Soviet Russian Literature, 1917–1950.* Norman: University of Oklahoma Press, 1951.

Swayze, Ernest Harold. "Soviet Literary Politics, 1946–1956." Unpublished doctoral dissertation, Harvard University, March 1958.

Trifonova, T. Review of *Not by Bread Alone*, in *Culture and Life*, January 1957, pp. 18–19.

Turkevich, John. "The Scientist in the U.S.S.R.," *Atlantic Monthly*, January 1958, pp. 45–49.

――――. "Soviet Science in the Post-Stalin Era," *Annals of the American Academy of Political and Social Science*, January 1956, pp. 139–151.

――――. "Soviet Science: Achievements and Problems," *Soviet Survey*, July–September 1959, pp. 38–43.

Vickery, Walter Neef. "Studies in Theoretical, Ideological, and Artistic Problems of Recent Soviet Literature." Unpublished doctoral dissertation, Harvard University, May 1958.

Volodin, Alexander. *A Factory Girl (Fabrichnaya devchonka)*, *Teatr*, September 1956.

Wilson, Edmund. "Doctor Life and His Guardian Angel" (review of *Doctor Zhivago*), in *New Yorker*, November 15, 1958, pp. 201–226.

Yashin, Alexander. "The Levers" ("Rychagi"), *Literaturnaya Moskva*, II. Moscow, 1956. Trans. by Miriam B. London in *Bitter Harvest*, ed. by Edmund Stillman. New York: Frederick A. Praeger, 1959.

Zhdanov, Nikolai. "A Trip Home" ("Poezdka na rodinu"), *Literaturnaya Moskva*, II. Moscow, 1956. Trans. by Elizabeth Marbury under the title "Journey Home" in *Bitter Harvest*, ed. by Edmund Stillman. New York: Frederick A. Praeger, 1959.

Zorin, Leonid. *The Guests (Gosti)*, *Teatr*, February 1954.

INDEX

When Boris Pasternak's *Doctor Zhivago* was published in Europe and America in 1957 and 1958, the Western world was astonished and elated. But *Doctor Zhivago* is not the only significant literary work to come out of Soviet Russia recently. During four extraordinary years, 1954 to 1957, from Stalin's death to the aftermath of the Hungarian revolt, Soviet Russian authors were able to express their minds with unusual freedom. In this volume Professor Gibian examines various revelations made in Soviet literature during this interval of comparative freedom.

Nearly a score of contemporary Soviet writers are considered in detail. The authors and their works are grouped according to three major subjects to which Soviet writers have devoted much attention: science, love and sex, and the literary villain or "ne ative" character.